Turning Point

The American Revolution → *in the* ← Spartan District

Katherine Cann

with GEORGE D. FIELDS JR.

First printing, October 2014

Editor: Betsy Wakefield Teter
Front cover design: Meg I. Reid
Cover photo of Blackstock's battlefield: Melissa Mellette
Book design: Brandy Lindsey and The Graphics House Inc.
Proofreaders: John Cribb, Jan Scalisi, Susan Thoms and Patrick Whitfill
Printed in Saline, MI by McNaughton & Gunn Inc.

Library of Congress Cataloging-in-Publication Data pending

186 West Main Street
Spartanburg SC 29306
864.577.9349
www.hubcity.org

DONORS

THE HUB CITY WRITERS PROJECT THANKS ITS friends who made contributions in support of this book and other Hub City programs.

Advance America

Mack and Patty Amick

Carol and Jim Bradof

Margaret Bridgforth

Martha Chapman

Stephen Colyer

Beth Cecil

Gail Ebert

Davis Enloe

Downtown Rotary Club

First Citizens Foundation

Inman Riverdale
  Foundation

Dorothy and Julian Josey

Mark and Sharon Koenig

Sara and Paul Lehner

David McCarthy

Carlin and Sander
  Morrison

Jeanie and Patrick
  O'Shaughnessy

Phifer/Johnson Foundation

Romill Foundation

Betty Snow

Sally and Warwick Spencer

Michel and Eliot Stone

South State Bank

South Carolina Arts
  Commission

John Lane and Betsy Teter

Billy and Lindsay Webster

The Art Lounge

Arkwright Foundation

Paula and Stan Baker

Brant and Judy Bynum

Sally and Jerry Cogan Jr.

Colonial Trust Company

Nancy Rainey Crowley

Eric and Brandy Lindsey

Deborah F. McAbee and J. Byron
  Morris

Dwight and Liz Patterson

Pat Tatham

Jimmy Wilson

Peter and Kathie Weisman

Mitch and Sarah Allen

Tom and Ceci Arthur

Robert and Susan Atkins

Andrew Babb

Don Bain

Tom and Joan Barnet

Valerie and Bill Barnet

John and Laura Bauknight

Cyndi and David Beacham

Charles and Christi Bebko

Pilley and Jay Bianchi

Victor and Linda Bilanchone

Don and Mott Bramblett

Walter and Dolores Brice

Bea Bruce

Myrna Bundy

Julia Burnett

Robert and Margaret Burnette

Dr. and Mrs. William W. Burns

Lynne and Bill Burton

Kathy and Marvin Cann

Donna R. Cart

Ruth Cate and Chuck White

Randall and Sally Chambers

Robert and Lacy Chapman

Jay Coffman and Keith Shambaugh

Rick and Sue Conner

Randall and Mary Lynn Conway

Celia and Randy Cooksey

Pamela Coppes

Nancy and Paul Cote

Tom Moore Craig

Dick and Ann Crenshaw

John and Kirsten Cribb

Garrow and Chris Crowley

Betsy Cox and Mike Curtis

Ken and Rachel Deems

Fredrick B. Dent

Magruder Dent

Elizabeth Drewry and Arthur
  Farwell III

Jean Dunbar

Kathy and Ray Dunleavy

William C. Elston

Edwin Epps

Jennifer and Alex Evins

Donald Fowler

ExxonMobil Foundation

Kerry and Mark Ferguson

George and Mildred Fields Jr.

First South Bank

Russel and Susan Floyd

Caleb and Delie Fort

Joan Foss

Steve and Abby Fowler

Larry and Betsy Fritz

Elaine T. Freeman

J. Sidney and Lenna Fulmer

Joan Gibson

Barney and Elaine Gosnell

Andrew Green

Lucy Grier

John Morton and Susan Griswold

Jim and Kay Gross

Roger and Marianna
  Habisreutinger

Benjy and Tanya Hamm

Al and Anita Hammerbeck

Bob and Barbara Hammett

Robert and Carolyn Harbison III

Darryl Harmon

John and Lou Ann Harrill Jr.

Peyton and Michele Harvey

Mark Hayes

David and Rita Heatherly

Stephanie Highsmith

Charlie Hodge

Holly Hoenig

Myrta and David Holt

Mr. and Mrs. Kenneth R. Huckaby

Joe and Elsa Hudson

Woody and Carol Hughes

Max Hyde

David and Harriet Ike

Susan Irwin

Sadie Jackson

Stewart and Ann Johnson

Wallace Eppes Johnson

Betsy and Charles Jones

Frannie Jordan

Daniel Kahrs

Peggy and Greg Karpick

Colleen Keith

Ann J. Kelly

Nancy Kenney

Thomas and Mimi Killoren

Beverly Knight

Bert and Ruth Knight

John M. Kohler Jr.

Connie Kunak

Mary Jane and Cecil Lanford

Jack and Kay Lawrence

Janice and Wood Lay

David Leavitt

George and Frances Loudon

Brownlee and Julie Lowry

Robert and Nancy Lyon

Ed and Suzan Mabry

Zerno Martin

Jim Mayo

Bill and Wendy Mayrose

John and Stacy McBride

John and Jill McBurney

North Carolina Writers Network

Byron McCane and Ellen Goldey

Betsy McGehee

Gayle Magruder

Kari and Phillip Mailloux

Larry E. Milan

Don and Mary Miles

Boyce and Carole Miller

Weston Milliken

Margot and Roger Milliken Jr.

Karen and Bob Mitchell

John and Belton Montgomery

Rick Mulkey and Susan Tekulve

Susan Myers

Neely Windows Doors and More

Margaret and George Nixon

Walter and Susan Novak

Corry and Amy Oakes

Geneva F. Padgett

Louise and W. Keith Parris

Richard Pennell

Sarah Chambers and Becky Pennell

Carolyn Pennell

Mr. and Mrs. Edward P. Perrin

Andrew and Mary Poliakoff

John and Lynne Poole

Jan and Sara Lynn Postma Jr.

Perrin and Kay Powell

Elizabeth and W.O. Pressley Jr.

Betty Price

Philip and Frances Racine

Rebecca Ramos

Eileen Rampey

Allison and John Ratterree

John Renfro

Rob Rhoden and Laura Barbas-
Rhoden

Naomi Richardson

Gail Rodgers

Elena and Steve Rush

J.B. Russell Construction Co.

Cate and Aaron Ryba

Mary Ann and Olin Sansbury

Kaye Savage

Susan Schneider

Garrett and Cathy Scott

Steve and Judy Sieg

Ruta Sepetys

Caroline and Ron Smith

Danny and Becky Smith

Lee and James Snell Jr.

Eugene and Rita Spiess

Hank and Marla Steinberg

Laura Stille

Tammy and David Stokes

Phillip Stone

Robert and Christine Swager

Frank Thies III

Ray E. Thompson Sr.

Deno Trakas

Jon Tuttle

Mark and Meredith Van Geison

Judith Waddell

Melissa Walker and Chuck Reback

Samantha Wallace

Bill and Winnie Walsh

Mary Ellen Wegrzyn

Brian Welsch

Dave and Linda Whisnant

Karen and John B. White Jr.

Floride Willard

Dennis and Anne Marie
Wiseman

Alanna and Don Wildman

Bob and Carolyn Wynn

CONTENTS

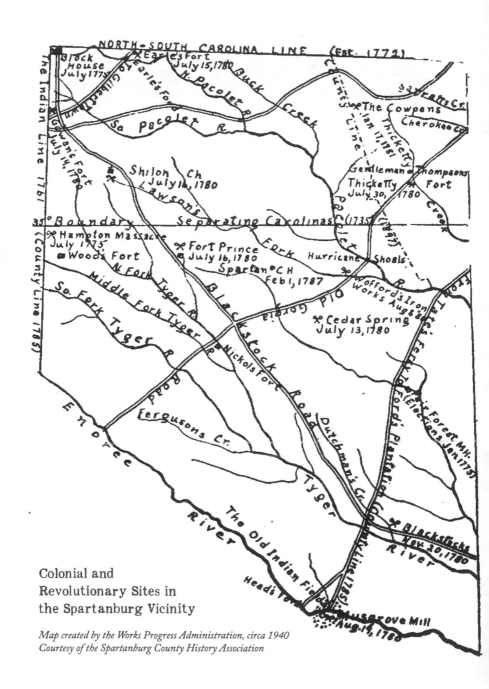

Colonial and
Revolutionary Sites in
the Spartanburg Vicinity

Map created by the Works Progress Administration, circa 1940
Courtesy of the Spartanburg County History Association

FOREWORD

Copperheads slither through the poison ivy that surrounds an old, unassuming building standing deep in a field near the bridge that spans Goucher Creek between Spartanburg and Gaffney. Trailing tendrils of kudzu threaten to consume the abandoned structure that is barely visible from the highway. The dilapidated structure gives no sign that it was part of Fort Thicketty, where men and women in the neighborhood sought protection from Native Americans in the mid-18th century. Nor is there anything to suggest that this was the site of an incredible drama that was unfolding more than two and a half centuries ago during the American Revolution.

In the summer of 1776, a group of brash American colonists dared to declare the 13 colonies independent of British rule, citing a litany of long-held grievances. The British attempted to crush the revolt, beginning in the Northeast where some Americans had been actively challenging British authority for more than a decade. By early 1780, it appeared the British intent to subdue all 13 colonies was going to succeed as they controlled all major ports but one (Charleston, South Carolina) and all important population centers.

However, they could not win a decisive military victory over the Continental Army commanded by George Washington.

Discouraged and frustrated, the British military turned to the South, believing the large population who remained loyal to the Crown would guarantee victory. In the spring of 1780, British forces drove the Patriot Provisional Government out of Charleston, South Carolina's only city and its capital. The South Carolina backcountry, including the Spartan District, had been relatively free of military action until after the fall of Charleston when the British and their Loyalist allies marched inland from the coast. From June 1780 until January 1781, the old Spartan District was a major area in the struggle for American independence. Most historians acknowledge that two key battles, Kings Mountain, just north of the Spartan District in York County, and Cowpens in the Spartan District, were decisive turning points in the War for American Independence.

Before these battles took place, however, from mid-summer 1780 until early winter 1781, more than a dozen engagements between Loyalists and Patriots occurred in the area between the Enoree and Broad rivers and along their major tributaries—the Tyger and the Pacolet. The road network in the area and its position between the upper piedmont and the mountains made control essential for both the Patriots and the British. The battles that summer in the Spartan District set the stage for significant British setbacks at Kings Mountain and Cowpens. They came at a crucial time in American history, and as a result, Patriot militiamen gained combat experience that proved vital to the American victories of late 1780 and early 1781. Most of these engagements were in present-day Spartanburg County. During that sequence of battles, Loyalist power in the area significantly diminished, one of the most successful and feared British commanders lost two battles, and the British major who had the task of rallying the Loyalists to the British cause died.

The Spartan District was part of the much larger Ninety Six Judicial District that included present-day Abbeville, Cherokee, Edgefield, Laurens, Newberry, Spartanburg, and Union counties. The northern area was the Upper Ninety Six or Spartan District. The number of people who lived in the Spartan District is unknown, but reached into the thousands. A majority of the residents were immigrants from Pennsylvania, Virginia, and North Carolina. They made a living as small farmers. A few of them undoubtedly relied on slave labor both for agricultural and construction work. Some of them were prosperous; most of them were not.

The unimpressive heart pine building on Thicketty Creek is the last standing structure in the area where military action occurred as American Patriots and Loyalists battled to control South Carolina. George D. Fields Jr., whose stories appear in this book as Fields' Notes, is a leader in the effort to preserve this remnant of Spartanburg County's Revolutionary War heritage. Fields, a former Methodist parish minister and former president of Spartanburg Methodist College, found his avocation in studying the American Revolution in the Spartanburg area. He has pored over historical accounts of the events and old and contemporary maps. He has tramped through fields, meadows and woods as he attempted to determine the exact site of battles and skirmishes long forgotten by most people. Committed to preserving the area's Revolutionary past, Fields contributed to the establishment of Musgrove Mill State Park and the purchase of the site of the Battle of Blackstock's, which is now a State Historic Site. He is currently working to preserve and restore the old building on the site of Fort Thicketty. His great knowledge of the Revolution in the Spartan District has been an invaluable resource in the preparation of this book.

Another individual who has spent much of his adult life studying the Revolution in the backcountry is my husband, Marvin Cann. Like George, Marvin worked diligently to preserve South Carolina's Revolutionary history and was a key player in securing National Historic Site status for the Ninety Six battle sites. Their contributions to this book cannot be measured. I also have relied on scholars and Revolutionary War enthusiasts who came before me; the notes acknowledge their works. My colleague at Spartanburg Methodist College, Dr. Harry Bayne, and Susan Thoms carefully read the manuscript and made suggestions that kept me from embarrassment. Betsy Teter of Hub City Press is an editor with a keen eye and a strong sense of what people want to read. Her recommendations strengthened the manuscript. Without the support of Spartanburg Methodist College, which gave me some release time from my instructional duties, I could not have completed this book. I owe these people and others many thanks.

Katherine

Katherine Cann
June 2014

Chapter 1

"What a Fair forest this"

Katherine Cann

For more than a half-century after the establishment of Charleston, the backcountry, a vast region lying 50 miles and more from the coast, was devoid of European settlers and only sparsely inhabited by Native Americans. The opening of the Great Wagon Road, which led south through piedmont valleys from Pennsylvania to Georgia, launched a migratory stream that significantly influenced the character of the emerging American nation. In the mid-19th century, hundreds of immigrants, perhaps disappointed with failure to acquire the land or the success they had left Europe to find, moved southward. Members of eight families from Lancaster County, Pennsylvania, arrived in the Spartan District in the mid-1750s. They were surprised and delighted to find "a beautiful valley" described by James McIlwaine: "[A] grove of lofty trees ... a meandering stream ... The rays of the declining sun shed their departing beams on the tree-tops that waved ... in the evening breeze. ... What a Fair forest this." The fortuitous setting, near where the Spartanburg/ Union County line crosses Fairforest Creek, must have seemed a good omen, for after camping along the creek, the McIlwaines and the others decided to make the area their home. Their settlement formed a nucleus around which other newcomers collected.

These eight families were among dozens who inched their way down the Great Wagon Road to South Carolina. The earliest immigrants arrived, not directly from Europe, but from Pennsylvania, Virginia, and North Carolina, along the route of the Great Wagon Road. They made their way south in cumbersome, wobbly wagons loaded down with household goods and farm implements.

When they arrived, the Spartan District was beyond the political, social, and economic bounds of South Carolina, then the wealthiest of England's North American colonies. It was the frontier, full of potential, but still in a natural state marked by hardwood forests, meandering streams, and gently rolling hills. Like other backcountry areas, the Spartan District was remote and only sparsely inhabited, an unorganized wilderness where Native Americans hunted and bandits roamed. Native Americans, mostly Cherokees, who were witnessing first-hand the loss of their lands to white settlement, made life in the backcountry dangerous and frightening.

Relations between South Carolina colonists and the native peoples were often strained and sometimes hostile. Yet in colonial South Carolina, the Cherokee trade was economically lucrative, and often unscrupulous traders trapped the Native Americans in debt, overcharged for shoddy merchandise, plied them with watered-down rum, and cheated them at every opportunity. The colonial government's efforts to regulate trade with Native American tribes failed to halt the serious abuses. The Cherokees, who regarded the Spartan District as their hunting ground, grew angry as white settlers intruded on tribal lands and ignored a boundary established in 1747.

Native American resentment of European settlement on traditionally tribal lands contributed to the Seven Years War. The war, a struggle for power between England and France, lasted from 1756 to 1763. Early in the conflict, Cherokee leaders supported Britain against France and welcomed construction of English forts to counter the threat of French expansion. In 1758, however, the Anglo-Cherokee alliance broke apart after a group of Virginia militiamen slaughtered a band of Cherokee warriors. In retaliation, the Cherokees and their Creek allies launched sporadic attacks along the frontier that brought the war to the Carolina backcountry.

Across the South Carolina backcountry, frightened settlers rushed to build forts for protection against Native American attacks. The backcountry forts were often crude, hastily constructed structures. More often than not, they surrounded a house and farm buildings on the property of leading families. Fort Thicketty in the eastern region of the Spartan District, Fort Prince near the Cherokee boundary line, and Earle's Fort and Gowen's Fort near the North Carolina border were among the places of refuge that offered settlers some protection from marauding Cherokees. All four of these structures were significant sites during the American Revolution.

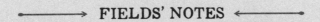

FIELDS' NOTES

"The early forts were practically windowless because those inside the fort did not want any access through which attackers could enter. Usually, the forts had only one small window on the back wall, opposite the door, on the chimney wall. Those in the fort knocked the chinking out between the logs in order to fire at the approaching enemy, so they did not need windows. At Earle's Ford, the Bayliss Earle family had buildings that could be a safe haven. The early forts proved their usefulness during the French and Indian War and also during the Cherokee War."

Cherokee raiders struck isolated settlers indiscriminately. At Long Canes, in the Ninety Six District about 75 miles from the settlers on Fairforest Creek, a vicious assault illustrated the danger posed by the Native Americans. On Sunday, February 1, 1760, a large band of Cherokees attacked 150 Long Canes settlers as they fled toward Augusta for safety. Among the 23 people killed and scalped were several members of the family of John C. Calhoun. The bodies were later buried in a common grave.

Continuing efforts to resolve the issues that divided settlers and Native Americans were disappointing. In 1761, British officials organized an expedition to Cherokee territory (now Tennessee) to subdue the Native Americans. As many as a thousand South Carolinians joined the expedition, characterized by skirmishes with the Native Americans, exhausting marches, and a scorched earth campaign that left Cherokee villages and fields in ashes. Members of the expedition burned 15 major villages and left 5,000 Cherokees facing starvation. British strategy distressed some of those who participated in the expedition. Francis Marion, a militia company commander, remembered: "'We proceeded ... to burn the Cherokee cabins. ... [T]o me it appeared a shocking sight. But when we came to cut down fields of corn, I could scarce refrain from tears. When we were gone, thought I, they would return and mark the ghastly ruin. . . . . [The children] will ask their mothers 'Who did this?' and the reply will be 'the White People did it –the Christians did it.'"

The tactics may have been distasteful, but the campaign ended Anglo-Cherokees hostilities for more than a decade. Moderate Cherokee leaders sued for peace, and negotiations resulted in a new Cherokee boundary 40 miles east of Keowee, the principal town of the Lower Cherokees. When it was surveyed, the boundary of Cherokee lands formed what became the dividing line between Greenville and Spartanburg counties, partly along Line Street in Greer.

The end of the Native American conflicts of the 1760s opened up new lands for European settlement, and an influx of white settlers moved into the Spartan District after the new boundary line had been established and the Native Americans had been pacified. By the late 1760s, a significant proportion of the colony's population lived in the backcountry where settlers found plentiful game, good springs, and well-established paths and trails leading towards Charleston. The climate, never too cold or too hot, with plentiful rainfall, was ideal for farming. In some areas, the soil was exceptionally rich and suitable for raising many crops. In others, stony clay soil enabled the cultivation of corn, wheat, rye and tobacco, which became the primary crops in the Spartan District. Shoals and fords in the swift-flowing rivers and streams presented spots where the waterways could easily be crossed. Those same streams and rivers offered plentiful water for crops and livestock. Falls, such as those on the Pacolet River, presented fishing opportunities and grist mill locations, and numerous springs offered home sites. Deciduous forests of oak, hickory, and chestnut supplied wood for cooking, construction, and warmth. An eye-catching bonus, the mountains about 50 miles distant, formed a scenic backdrop to the rolling hills of the region.

Many of the newcomers were Scots-Irish, men and women of English and Scot ancestry who came to America in great numbers from northern Ireland where their ancestors had been resettled more than a century before by order of the Crown. By the 1760s, the Scots-Irish faced increased rents, high taxes, and devastating drought that pushed farmers off the land. Many of them were "beggared and some had died without food or shelter." The Scots-Irish, most of whom were Presbyterian, stood by helplessly in Northern Ireland as the Anglican Church threatened to overwhelm Presbyterianism. Letters from America tempted them with news of inexpensive land, religious freedom, and a brighter future. Some Presbyterian ministers in Ireland encouraged entire congregations to pool their money and move to America, where they could live as free men and women. Many took their words to heart, including the Chesney family, who joined some of their relatives already living at Grindal Shoals on the Pacolet River near present-day Jonesville in 1772. The ocean voyage was especially arduous for the Chesneys due to an outbreak of smallpox on the ship. Crowded conditions on board fueled the spread of the disease, and when the ship docked at Charleston, the government quarantined the passengers for several months.

Among the newcomers at this time were members of the Earle family, who came from Virginia in 1768 and lived on the North Pacolet River near the mountains. By the time of the Revolution, Bayliss Earle operated Earle's Ford on the Pacolet River, the site of a shallow river crossing. The Princes, their friends, neighbors, and in-laws, settled on Gray's Creek, a tributary of the North Tyger River. John and Jane Thomas came to Fishing Creek on the Catawba River, on Native American land, before settling near the confluence of Fairforest and Kelso Creeks in 1762. The Scots-Irish Moore family had emigrated from Ireland to Pennsylvania and then to North Carolina. Charles Moore, his wife, and eight children settled a land grant along the Tyger River and its tributaries, and established Walnut Grove Plantation. Thomas Fletchall had established a plantation on Fairforest Creek near the present day city of Union, about

1760. He acquired 1,600 acres of land on which he built a gristmill and raised grain and livestock. The Hamptons, perhaps somewhat more daring, moved from North Carolina to within sight of the Cherokee boundary in 1773.

FIELDS' NOTES

"It is surprising how many settlers lived along the creeks in the Spartan District. Almost all of them farmed 40 to 50 acres, so there were many cabins along the creeks and roads. The principal way they earned a living was agriculture. There were some ironworks here then, but farmers made their living from the land. The principal crop, other than food for themselves and their livestock, was tobacco. Few families were wealthy like the Moores, who owned Walnut Grove. A high percentage of people in this section had moved in here after 1775. South Carolina conducted a census in 1775 to see what its manpower was for the war. It showed only 7,500 males of militia age who could fight. The big migration into this area happened between 1775 and 1780."

With cultural traditions developed in Europe, families such as the Chesneys and the Moores found the American environment reminiscent of the land that they had been compelled to leave. The geography of the South Carolina backcountry was particularly suited to small-scale family farming, the livelihood of most of the Scots-Irish. Reportedly, among the Scots-Irish immigrants, "no more than one in ten were men of substance," or the "provincial gentry" that included the well-known Calhoun, Jackson, Moore, and Fletchall families. Their fiercely independent spirit, resentment of authority, and the value they placed on family may have developed from living in the midst of Irishmen who posed a constant threat.

The new arrivals put down their roots near the Pacolet, Enoree, and Tyger rivers and on the creeks, including Thicketty, Fairforest, and Lawson's Fork. The men constructed log cabins, a distinctive architectural contribution of the Carolina Scots-Irish to frontier life, consisting of one room where an entire family lived. The floor was dirt and the windows little more than holes in the walls. Those who were perhaps more optimistic, or richer, or more energetic might choose to build a "dog-trot" cabin that connected two side-by-side log structures separated by an open breezeway. By the time of the American Revolution, the Scots-Irish had become the second-largest ethnic group in the American colonies. Their contributions to the evolving national character and the American Revolution were substantial.

From the beginning, backcountry settlers disliked the planter elite who controlled South Carolina economically and politically. Although colonial officials encouraged Scots-Irish settlement of the backcountry, they scorned Scots-Irish folkways, tendency to violence, wariness of strangers, and religious practices. They hoped that a larger population in the backcountry would protect the more established, wealthier coastal region from the Native Americans and provide manpower in the event of a slave revolt. Neither town merchants, nor the royal government in Charleston, nor the planter elite accepted the backcountry yeomen as equals. Charles Woodmason, an Anglican cleric from Charleston, thought most of the backcountry residents were the "Scum of the Earth and the Refuse of mankind." The people, wrote a horrified Woodmason, lived in "open log cabins with hardly a blanket to cover them." Colonel George Hanger, a Loyalist, thought the hardy, hard-working Scots-Irish were "more savage than the Native Americans and possess every one of their vices and not one of their virtues." Even the Revolutionary period South Carolina governor, John Rutledge, thought the Scots-

Irish who inhabited the frontier regions of his state were a "pack of beggars . . . belligerent, loyal, bigoted, valiant, crude and rough. The men drank hard and families moved often. Their young women shocked sensibilities with public displays of bosoms and legs." Though disdained by the elite, during the Native American wars and the Revolution, the Scots-Irish attributes that Rutledge noted—belligerence, loyalty, bravery—served the people of South Carolina well. They were men and women who "might bend but never break."

Eighteenth-century life in the South Carolina backcountry was not for the weak or cosseted. Immigrants often came in family groups, which made everyday life easier, afforded a sense of community, and offered a measure of protection from the perils of frontier life. Relatively isolated from sources of essential supplies, backcountry settlers were largely self-sufficient and cultivated flax for cloth, as well as various food crops. Many raised hogs and cattle, and most had at least one horse. Few industrial sites had developed in the Spartan District by the time of the Revolution except for the ironworks on Lawson's Fork, near present-day Glendale. The ironworks was established by William Wofford and Joseph Buffington with assistance from the Provincial Congress, which was interested in supporting the Revolutionary War effort. After purchasing

Buffington's interest, Wofford operated the business, producing bar iron. It was one of the major South Carolina ironworks. Once the Revolution was underway, Wofford's Ironworks had become a commercial center and produced horseshoes and weapons used by the Patriots.

The lowcountry Anglican elite had no more respect for backcountry religions than for backcountry settlers. Backcountry Presbyterians looked upon Anglican clergymen as "black-gowned sons of bitches." Contrary to the perception of Charleston dandies, who seemed to think the backcountry was filled with immoral, ungodly people, the folks who lived there took religion seriously, establishing congregations and making the "best arrangements in their power for the worship of the God of their fathers." On the frontier, attracting a university-educated minister, required by the Presbyterian Church, was difficult. Church buildings were remote and services irregular. Yet many families maintained their religious customs and tenets even in the absence of ordained ministers and regular services. The people, according to some sources, "were not roughnecks nor ignoramuses" and "excelled in all the virtues of the Christian and the man."

For nearly a decade, Presbyterians in the Tyger River vicinity worshipped informally in homes. By 1767, a group of churchmen living near the Tyger River, including the family of Charles Moore, had organized a congregation. In 1772, the congregation erected a proper church and named Joseph Alexander as minister; he served the congregation until after the Revolution. Soon, Nazareth Church was the largest Presbyterian church in what is now Spartanburg County.

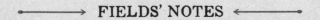 **FIELDS' NOTES**

"The Baptists at that time were not like Southern Baptists of today. In Northern Ireland, the Presbyterians had a rule that you had to have a university-trained pastor. But the backcountry congregations were so poor they could not pay one, so they reorganized as Baptist churches so they could ordain their own pastors who had no university training. The theology was very similar to that of the Presbyterian Church. When the war began, South Carolina leaders in Charleston began to discuss abolishing the Anglican Church as the established church because they thought the backcountry people would not support the new Patriot state without a movement to do away with the established church."

While many of the Scots-Irish embraced some brand of Presbyterianism, Baptists, an even more diverse group, also could be found in many backcountry settlements. Though the number of Baptists in colonial South Carolina was relatively small, a number of them lived in the area between the Broad and Saluda rivers. Many of the Baptists in the Spartan District belonged to the branch of Baptists called New Lights or Separates. Plain and simple people, the Separates took their religious beliefs directly from the New Testament and disapproved of behavior such as adultery, drunkenness, and fighting. They did not always get along with their fellow Baptists or the Presbyterians among whom they lived. The Separates invited ridicule due to their "uneducated preachers, female participation in church services, and . . . foot washing." In many ways, this group of Baptists suited the disposition of those backcountry settlers who tended to be suspicious of formal religious authority.

Philip Mulkey, the best-known and most influential Baptist preacher in the backcountry, came to the Spartan District from North Carolina in 1759-60 with members of his congregation. He soon acquired property on Fairforest Creek, where he established a church, the first Baptist church in the South Carolina backcountry. Preachers associated with the church on Fairforest Creek also organized congregations at Thicketty, Goshen (Goucher), and Enoree in the early 1770s. By the time of the Revolution, Mulkey's following consisted of as many as 400 souls. Mulkey was reputedly a gifted speaker, and people paid attention to his words on politics as well as religion. According to a critic, he "came here lately in Rags, hungry and barefoot [and] can now, at his beck or Nod, or Motion of his finger lead out four Hundred men into the Wilderness in a Moment, at his speaking the word."

Social and religious differences were two of many issues that alienated the men and women of the backcountry from the seat of power in Charleston. Furthermore, all legal transactions, from criminal cases to recording deeds, took place only in Charleston. In the absence of sheriffs and courts, the people of the backcountry depended on the colonial government in Charleston to protect property and maintain civic order. Colonial officials, however, lacked the resources and interest to tackle the problems in the interior.

Living more than 200 miles from Charleston, frontier settlers often found themselves targets of Native American raiders. The colonial government, which included no representatives from the backcountry, had attempted to subdue the Native Americans during the Cherokee War, but raids and attacks continued to plague the region. In the absence of local law enforcement, backcountry settlers also had to worry about robbers and outlaw gangs that included women and escaped slaves who roamed the area, plundering and murdering with impunity and without fear of capture.

The colonial government's failure to take action against this crime wave led desperate settlers in the backcountry to take matters into their own hands. The result was the Regulator Movement of 1767. As many as 1,000 men from the backcountry pledged to "execute the laws" against criminals and to support each other in times of danger. They were mostly small farmers who aimed "to civilize" the region with their vigilante actions. Wealthier residents, if not actually part of the movement, supported it, hoping that ending the reckless disorder would create a safe environment for commercial activity, plantation agriculture, and the expansion of slavery.

The Regulator Movement dramatized the conflict between the backcountry and the coast. Late in 1767, the Regulators presented a petition to the Commons House of

Assembly, the colony's legislature in Charleston, demanding establishment of backcountry courts, construction of courthouses and jails, schools, restrictions on poachers, and the enactment of more stringent laws against "idleness and vice." During the next few months, the Regulators killed a number of outlaws, captured others, and sent them to Charleston for trial. The Regulators then turned their attention to squatters, petty thieves, and poachers and banished them from the settlements.

The colonial government sent two well-armed mounted Ranger units, whose members came mostly from the coastal region, into the backcountry. Joined by some of the Regulators, the Rangers quickly crushed the remaining outlaw gangs using tactics ranging from whipping to hanging. In the wake of the Regulator Movement, the colonial government also attempted to address other concerns of the backcountry. In 1769, the Commons House of Assembly passed a law establishing courts and jails, and appointing sheriffs in six backcountry districts. The Ninety Six judicial district encompassed the area between the Enoree and Broad rivers and included the Spartan District. Judges sent from England by the Crown began holding court at Ninety Six in late 1772.

Hoping to preserve stability in the interior, the Provincial Government reorganized the Provincial Regiment, a local militia unit of indeterminate size commanded by a colonel, in 1775. As a result of the changes, seven of 12 Colonial Militia regiments came from non-coastal regions, two of them from the area between the Broad and Saluda rivers. The Provincial Government appointed colonels and majors while the regiment selected lower-grade officers. Thomas Fletchall, the commander of the militia in that entire area, became colonel of the Upper Militia Regiment that comprised all of the Spartan District.

Although a measure of law and order returned to the region, tension between the Regulators and other settlers persisted. Bitter feuds that pitted individuals and communities against each other foreshadowed the civil war of the Revolutionary era. Some of these disputes and quarrels carried over into the next decade.

Chapter 2

"To Live in Peace and True Friendship With Our Neighbors"

The decade between 1773 and 1783 was a significant time in South Carolina and the evolving American nation. Troubles over taxes and other issues escalated into more violent protests and, by 1775, a full-scale war. From July 1780 until January 1781, the Spartan District was a key area in the struggle for American independence. Major roads traversed the Spartan District, creating a transportation network that was valuable for both Patriot and Loyalist military tactics. Blackstock Road, the oldest in the region, originated as a Native American path that led through the district to Ninety Six. There it linked with roads to Charleston and Augusta. The Georgia Road connected in Charlotte with the Great Wagon Road through Virginia and ultimately to Philadelphia. Another east/west road, the Green River Road, led from a crossing on the Broad River in present-day York County to the Green River region in North Carolina and then into Cherokee country.

Relatively small battles in the Spartan District in late 1780 contributed to the destruction of Loyalist power in South Carolina, and the Battle of Cowpens in January 1781 drove the Loyalists out of this area. A second phase in the Patriot conquest of South Carolina occurred when General Nathanael Greene brought the Continental Army back to South Carolina and Lord Charles Cornwallis began the fateful march to Yorktown. The British struggle to win South Carolina ended when Cornwallis left. The third phase of the war shifted to other areas in the colonies, but the militia regiments from the Spartan District continued to fight Loyalists through a long campaign that culminated in the British surrender at Yorktown and the evacuation of the British military from South Carolina.

FIELDS' NOTES

"Much of the fighting in July and August 1780 occurred on the Georgia and Blackstock Roads. Heritage has it that the British buried soldiers slain in battle where they fell. The militia generally took bodies home as they left the field of battle. On hot summer days, the militia might have also buried their fallen on site. The story goes that a British soldier picked some peaches from trees on the side of the road but died in battle before he could eat them. Some of the seeds sprouted and took root, leading some to call one of the skirmishes the Battle of the Peach Trees."

The First Continental Congress, elected in the summer of 1774 to represent most of the 13 colonies, met in Philadelphia to discuss taking measures against what they regarded as British intrusion in colonial affairs. The Continental Congress approved the Articles of Association that included a pledge to support the boycott of British goods. In January 1775, a group of about 200 South Carolinians declared themselves to be a Provincial Congress. Their action challenged British government and authority in the province, setting in motion the break between the colonies and England that occurred the following year. Two months after the skirmish at Lexington and Concord, in June 1775, the Provincial Congress in Charleston joined other colonies in embracing the Articles of Association, commonly called the Association, recognizing the authority of the Provincial Congress, and "defending South Carolina against every foe . . . until a reconciliation shall take place between Great Britain and America . . ." While this congress purported to represent the people of South Carolina, only 40 of the 189 representatives came from the backcountry, home to three-fourths of the colony's population. The Revolutionary-era government in South Carolina, consisting of three administrative committees, included the 13-member

Council of Safety, which had supreme military authority and served as an executive committee of the Provincial Government.

At once, in anticipation of armed confrontation with England, the Council of Safety organized a military force comprised of three Patriot militia regiments—two line regiments from the coastal region and a regiment of mounted infantry in the backcountry. The militiamen were local volunteers who, during the American Revolution, usually served indefinite terms of enlistment. Several militia units acting together formed a regiment, commanded by a colonel. Other militia companies could be organized as circumstances required. These three Patriot regiments were a part of the Continental Army, commanded by George Washington and established by the Continental Congress that was acting as the government in the 13 colonies.

Persuading members of the royal militia to support the Patriot cause was a vital element in the council's plan. The royal militia, consisting of approximately 12,000 men, had been formed to protect the population from Native American attacks. However, the loyalties of this force were uncertain. Many of the militiamen in the Spartan District were reluctant to support the new government as they had good reasons for their allegiance to the Crown. They were grateful for the land grants they had received from the British government. Issues with England that so vexed those who lived on the coast—taxes on imported goods, the appointment of civil officials, and the meddling in legislative affairs by royal governors—had little import in the backcountry, where a majority had no desire to exchange British rule for the "petty tyrannies being spawned by the rebellion." Many looked to local religious and political leaders for guidance. Consequently, both the King's friends and Patriot leaders vied for the support of prominent colonists in the backcountry.

In the summer of 1775, reports from the backcountry suggested strong opposition to the Provincial Government in Charleston and its challenges to British authority. Bad blood between backcountry Loyalists and Patriots that had been festering for a while became more heated after Loyalists successfully raided Ninety Six, the location of the jail and courthouse and the center of British authority in the backcountry. Thomas Fletchall, the most prominent Loyalist in the area, was a militia officer, magistrate, and coroner. His influence with local militiamen could boost the Provincial Government's authority in the Spartan District. The Patriots tried to win over Fletchall by offering an appointment to a committee to enforce the anti-British boycott, but he refused. Although Fletchall realized that failure to support the Provincial Congress would likely cost him his militia commission, he remained steadfast in his loyalty to the Crown. When the Council of Safety urged Fletchall to muster his regiment in order to give the men an opportunity to support the Association, he did so. However, he did not encourage his troops to join the Patriot cause and refused to do so himself; not one of the thousand or so militiamen in Fletchall's regiment signed. Instead, many of them endorsed a separate document saying they saw no reason to reject the Crown's authority. Their signatures constituted a promise to live in "peace and true friendship" with their neighbors. As it turned out, this promise was short-lived.

With this failure to gain Fletchall's conversion, Patriot leaders in Charleston worried that support for the Loyalist position was increasing in the backcountry. Once more, in August 1775, the Council of Safety attempted to sway popular sentiment to the Patriot cause, and sent a commission to the disaffected backcountry. William Henry Drayton, a prominent member of the new Provincial Government and representative of the lowcountry elite, led the delegation. Drayton, once a devotee of the Crown, had become a "zealous champion of the new cause" and was known in the Spartan District where he owned an interest in an ironworks. William Tennant, member of the General Assembly and minister at Charleston's Independent (Presbyterian) Church, and Oliver Hart, the most prominent Baptist preacher in South Carolina who served the Baptist Church in Charleston, accompanied Drayton. These two men echoed the religious sensibilities of most of the backcountry residents. Richard Richardson, a wealthy planter and militia colonel from Camden, and Joseph Kershaw, a prosperous merchant also from Camden, rounded out the five-man commission. Joseph McJunkin, who lived near the Tyger River in the eastern part of the Spartan District, served as their guide. The commissioners' purpose was to explain the issues that led to the formation of the provisional government and enlist support for the Patriot government and the Association. The Council of Safety impressed upon the commissioners the need to emphasize that only a "general union" would protect the people from "slavery" to the imperial government. The commissioners hoped to convince all militia officers to join the Association. Presumably they, in turn, could persuade the men in their regiments to do the same. This delicate task was particularly significant as the militia were the key to the Council of Safety's military plans.

The commissioners held mass meetings as they wound their way through the backcountry. These gatherings combined elements of political rhetoric and evangelical fervor, often taking on the characteristics of a revival. Traveling separately for the most part, the commissioners cut a wide swath through the backcountry from the Congarees near present-day Columbia, to the German settlements around Saxe Gotha at the confluence of the Broad and Saluda rivers near modern Lexington, to the Scots-Irish settlements near Lawson's Fork and Fairforest Creek. Many in the backcountry found it difficult to trust Drayton, a wealthy man from Charleston whose interests seemed different from their own. This attitude complicated the commissioners' six-week mission that began in early August 1775.

At Thicketty Creek meeting house, preaching to a Scots-Irish audience, Tennant and Hart demonstrated their value as commission members. Members of several Baptist congregations in the vicinity of Fort Thicketty and Grindal Shoals gathered to hear the commissioners' message. Tennant addressed the crowd for two hours before refreshing himself by drinking water from a cowbell. The address must have been powerful and persuasive, because most of these present signed the Association document.

On August 11, Reverend Hart addressed about 30 people at Fairforest Baptist Church, pastored by Philip Mulkey. Hart reported that Mulkey's congregation knew "but little about the Matter" yet remained so firmly loyal to England "that no argument . . . seemed to have any Weight with them." Members of the small crowd warned Hart that the situation in the area was growing dangerous, as the inhabitants were taking sides and a civil war loomed. Some in the group were outright hostile toward the Patriots. Aware of events that had occurred in Massachusetts the previous April, one Loyalist in the congregation declared that he would like to see a thousand Bostonians killed. The listeners' loyalty to the Crown was unmistakable.

A week later, on August 17, the commissioners approached Colonel Thomas Fletchall. Drayton observed that, despite his prominence, many people in the area did not like him and was optimistic that a recruitment effort at Fletchall's plantation might meet with some success. A three-hour audience with Fletchall, whom Drayton called a "great and mighty nabob," did nothing to change the colonel's point of view. But he did agree to call a muster at

John Ford's plantation on the Enoree River, where Drayton could give his spiel in favor of resistance to British policies. The decidedly unfriendly mood of the crowd at Ford's disappointed Drayton. Few militiamen showed up, and although about 70 signed the Association, Drayton thought most of them "were our friends" from other places.

On August 21, Drayton and Hart received an enthusiastic reception complete with a barbeque at Captain Joseph Wofford's on Lawson's Fork near the ironworks and the Cherokee boundary line. Both Hart and Drayton addressed an attentive crowd that day. According to Drayton, the people were "active and spirited. They are staunch in our favor." The Charlestonian optimistically predicted that eventually "this whole frontier will be formed into voluntary companies," but at the time, most men still sided with Fletchall.

John Thomas Sr. was among those who heard Drayton and Hart speak at Wofford's. The commissioners met with Thomas and others at his home near the junction of Fairforest and Kelso creeks. Thomas was a respected figure in the Spartan District, a magistrate who had been a captain in the royal militia unit. In that capacity, he fought in the French and Indian War but had resigned his commission in the early 1770s. Persuaded by the commissioners, Thomas began to believe "the malignants are forming the most hellish schemes to frustrate the measures of the Continental Congress, and to use all those who are willing to stand by those measures in the most cruel manner." He promised to raise a regiment to support the Provincial Government. However, as he acknowledged, many potential militiamen might be reluctant to leave their families alone and unprotected in the event of hostilities. This new Spartan Regiment, a Patriot unit, was the counterpart to the royal militia force commanded by Fletchall. By September, the two regiments in the Spartan District, both commanded by highly esteemed men, John Thomas Sr. and Thomas Fletchall, competed for the hearts and minds of the people who lived in the area between the Enoree and Broad rivers.

While Drayton's speeches may have inspired some to sign on with the Patriots, they drove others away, and Loyalist militia numbers grew in the Spartan District. Frustrated by the lack of support in the backcountry, Drayton was increasingly belligerent, threatening to march against the Loyalists with a military force and cannon. He devised a ruse calculated to encourage Fletchall to change his mind. He ordered Thomas and the Spartan Regiment to destroy the homes of those who had not signed the Association and were away from home. Then, Drayton ensured that Loyalists intercepted the orders and learned of the plan. Next, he invited Fletchall to participate in a conference at Ninety Six, accompanied by some of his most prominent neighbors, including militia captains John Ford and Benjamin Wofford. The Rev. Mulkey, who had been outspoken in his strong support for England, also joined the group that met with Drayton in mid-September 1775 at Ninety Six hoping to forestall civil war.

The meeting belonged to Drayton and the Patriots. Fletchall had no appetite for a fight and did not take much of a stand for the Loyalists. In the agreement called the Treaty of Ninety Six, the Loyalists promised to live in "peace and tranquility" and never to "aid, assist or join" any British troops. They also recognized the Council of Safety's authority to arrest or imprison any person who criticized or opposed the Provincial Government. In turn, the Patriots guaranteed the "lives, persons and property" of the backcountry Loyalists. Uncertain of British support should hostilities develop, Fletchall got so drunk that he was unaware of his actions as he endorsed the agreement. Many, but not all, of his delegation refused to follow his example. The Treaty of Ninety Six established a brief and uneasy peace.

FIELDS' NOTES

"Three things brought the Patriots together. The only organized institution in this area was the church. And the Presbyterians and Baptist Church had connections all the way up the wagon road to Philadelphia. In 1775, the Presbyterian Church headquartered in Pennsylvania had five missionaries in South Carolina. Many of the Presbyterian churches in the upcountry of South Carolina emerged from the work of these missionaries. The church was the only institution left when government collapsed.

Secondly, commercial ties connected people who traded up and down the wagon road. Third was a family connection. These three things took the place of the Provincial Government when the British took Charleston in 1780."

In the event of a war with England, Patriot success depended upon Native American neutrality. Drayton, hoping to break the Anglo-Cherokee alliance, had conferred with Cherokee headmen to assure them they need not fear the new Provisional Government and promised to provide powder and lead for the winter hunt. Thinking the Cherokees had been placated, the Council of Safety hired a wagoner to deliver powder and lead to the Cherokee towns from Ninety Six, where they had been stored in the dungeon of the jail. Events that followed, however, surprised and stunned the Patriots. The Native American trader Richard Pearis, a Patriot turned Loyalist, planted a rumor that the Council of Safety meant the ammunition to be used by the Cherokees against Loyalist settlers in the interior. Less than 20 miles from Ninety Six, a group of about 150 Loyalists waylaid the shipment and seized the contents in the name of the King. They appropriated the powder and cut the lead into small pieces on the spot. The Loyalist force, now much better armed, set up camp and recruited new members until their numbers grew to almost 2,000 men.

The Patriots in Ninety Six were determined to recover the powder. Believing the Loyalists planned to use their expanded force to attack the fort at Ninety Six, Patriot militiamen led by Colonel Andrew Williamson hastily erected a crude fort across a ravine from the Ninety Six jail. The next day, November 19, 1775, the Loyalists arrived, many of them from the Spartan District, and demanded the fort's surrender. For two and a half days, these two opposing groups of American militiamen exchanged gunfire, with neither side overwhelming the other. The first battle at Ninety Six ended late on November 22 with a cease fire. The Patriots destroyed their fort; the Loyalists agreed to withdraw beyond the Saluda River. Both sides would free prisoners taken earlier in the month. At the last minute, the Loyalists insisted the Patriots relinquish their swivel guns, and the Loyalists moved these light cannon to Fort Charlotte near Augusta. The action at Ninety Six in November 1775 brought the Revolution to the South; it was the first military encounter outside of New England.

But the hostilities did not end on November 22. The Royal Governor, Lord William Campbell, had already bolted South Carolina, leaving the Provincial Congress the only government in the colony. At the end of November, the Provincial Congress dispatched a large army into the backcountry. Composed of South and North Carolina militiamen and recruits in the newly formed Continental Army, the force's objective was to stamp out Loyalist opposition to the Revolutionary regime. In December 1775, the Patriots in John Thomas's Spartan Regiment saw their first action as part of this much larger Patriot force, numbering as many as 5,000. The Patriots surprised the last remaining Loyalist unit at the Great Cane Brake on the Reedy River in Cherokee territory. During a storm in which 30 inches of snow fell, the Patriot army captured more than 100 Loyalists, including Thomas Fletchall, Benjamin Wofford, and Richard Pearis. They remained imprisoned in Charleston until July 1776. Most Loyalists who agreed to end their opposition to the Provincial Government were paroled. Some Loyalists agreed to sign a pledge promising never to take up arms against the Patriots, but others fled the province, seeking refuge in Native American territory or in East Florida.

After this Snow Campaign, the Patriots and Provincial Government controlled South Carolina. In February 1776, the Provincial Congress divided the large area between the Broad and Saluda rivers into three election and regimental districts. The Upper District was called the Spartan District. The following month, long before the Continental Congress announced the Declaration of Independence, South Carolina became the second state to create a constitution, and the newly elected General Assembly replaced the Provincial Congress as South Carolina's governing body. In the backcountry, animosity between Patriots and Loyalists became more heated, and the political issues that originally divided them "were gradually lost in the confusion of Native American raids, massacres, family feuds, and plain banditry."

Expecting the British to attack and fearing that they

might incite the Cherokees against backcountry settlers, the General Assembly made plans to defend the colony. A celebrated battle on Sullivan's Island late in June 1776 thwarted the initial British invasion, and the remnants of the royal government evacuated Charleston. The next month, encouraged by British agents, the Cherokees went on the warpath in the backcountry.

FIELDS' NOTES

"The British had planned a two-pronged attack in South Carolina. One was a naval attack on Sullivan's Island, now Fort Moultrie, near Charleston. The other prong was a Cherokee attack across the Cherokee boundary, now the Greenville-Spartanburg County line. That is where South Carolina ended, which meant this part of South Carolina in that particular period was an intense combat zone. Most of the battles in that period in the Spartan District were around what they called the Native American frontier forts, which had been built by settlers as forts of refuge where they could seek safety in the event of a Native American attack."

South Carolina colonists thought they had seen the last of the Native American peril. However, events in 1776 proved them wrong and reiterated the dangers of frontier life when Cherokee warriors indiscriminately attacked backcountry settlements. Both Patriots and Loyalists suffered in the brutal conflict. The South Carolina attacks were part of a widespread Cherokee uprising intended to end European incursions into Cherokee lands all along the southern frontier. The heaviest blow occurred in South Carolina, where frightened settlers sought safety in isolated frontier forts to escape death. On the upper reaches of the Pacolet River in North Carolina, a Native American war party attacked the Hannon family in the spring of 1776. Three children who survived the attack walked along the river until they reached Colonel Bayliss Earle's house in the Spartan District, where other neighbors had found refuge from the Cherokees.

The worst attack in the Spartan District occurred when a Cherokee band massacred members of the Hampton family before they could find safety at nearby Wood's Fort. Anthony Hampton and his family had moved from Virginia to settle in the Spartan District the early 1770s near the Cherokee boundary line. One of the five Hampton sons, Preston, was a Native American trader. On a summer day in 1776, a band of Cherokees approached the Hampton home. The Hamptons sent some of the children to warn their neighbors who were also relatives. According to an early account: "*Old Mr. Hampton, it is said, met the Indians cordially. He gave the chief a friendly grasp of the hand, but had not more than done this when he saw his son, Preston, fall from the fire of a gun. The same hand which he had grasped a moment before sent a tomahawk through his skull. In the same way his wife was killed. An infant . . . was dashed against the wall of the house, which was spattered with its blood and brains. The Indians then set fire to the house of Mr. Hampton. Mrs. Hampton, on coming up, seeing her father's house in flames, came very near rushing into the midst of the savages. Her husband, anticipating what the trouble was, held her back until the savages were gone.*" According to one story, when the survivors reached Wood's Fort, near a tributary of the Tyger River called Hampton Branch, some time later, the commandant did not believe their story, thinking that no Cherokees were on the warpath at the time. Finally persuaded that an attack had occurred, some of the fort's garrison went to the Hampton farm and found the mutilated bodies. Edward Hampton, away from home at the time of the massacre, survived.

Colonel Andrew Williamson, Patriot commander of the Ninety Six District, assembled an army of nearly

2,000 backcountry militia, including most of the Spartan Regiment, to drive the Cherokees back to the Lower Towns near Keowee. The force included both Loyalists and Patriots who, in the face of a common enemy, put aside their political differences. Alexander Chesney, for example, a Loyalist who lived on the Pacolet River, and Andrew Barry, a Patriot who lived at Walnut Grove, both joined Williamson's militia. In a campaign that lasted several months, Williamson's men destroyed the Lower Cherokee Towns and inflicted great damage to the Cherokees and their territory. This was one of several successful campaigns against the Native Americans that ended the threat of raids and attacks. In May 1777, the Cherokees agreed to the terms of the Treaty of Dewitt's Corner, surrendering all their lands in South Carolina, except a small corner of present-day Oconee County, and withdrawing to the mountains of North Carolina and Tennessee.

And so, in 1777, peace came to the Spartan District. Or did it? The British were gone. The Native Americans subdued. The Loyalists tamed. The Revolution continued in the middle colonies and New England. But in the South, hostility between those who advocated independence and those who hoped for a return to imperial rule intensified, and open warfare would flare up once more.

"The British forces were mainly Provincials, that is, Americans trained to British army specifications. Most were from New York and New Jersey. They were sent south to fight, and constituted the major British military force. Major Patrick Ferguson was the only British regular army officer in the Spartan District. British General Henry Clinton appointed Ferguson to command the Loyalist units in the upcountry. He quickly began to establish a series of control points throughout the Spartan District. His major headquarters was on a shoals on Fairforest Creek, near the present-day town of Union. Moving up the old Blackstock Road, Ferguson established a series of forts, including Musgrove Mill, Fort Prince (near Fairforest), Gowen's Old Fort (near Gowensville), and Fort Thicketty in what is now Cherokee County."

In June 1778, when the British evacuated Philadelphia, they began a concerted effort to recover the southern colonies. This strategy that depended on mobilizing British sympathizers in the region gave new hope to Loyalists who had been biding their time in anticipation of an eventual return to royal rule. Passions were intense on both sides.

On February 14, 1780, a detachment of South Carolina Patriots, led by Colonels Andrew Pickens and Elijah Clark, met a Loyalist militia force en route to Augusta at Kettle Creek in Georgia, barely across the Savannah River near the current town of Washington. Pickens's smaller force easily overwhelmed the Loyalists, who were caught by surprise. The victorious Patriots marched 75 prisoners to Ninety Six. After a trial, most were condemned to death, but eventually only five were hanged. The harsh result of the trial, coupled with the humiliating defeat at Kettle Creek, fueled anti-Patriot sentiments and reprisals throughout the South Carolina backcountry that persisted for the duration of the war.

FIELDS' NOTES

"The failure of the Southern Strategy may have resulted from British disdain of colonists. In the Loyalists' journals it appears that the British treatment of them was terrible. In many cases they were not respected, like when Banastre Tarleton was chasing Thomas Sumter before the battle at Blackstock's. Sumter had something like 80 or 90 Loyalist militiamen that he had captured down in what is now Newberry and Laurens County where he was maneuvering while Tarleton was chasing him. Tarleton killed most of the captives, attacking them without clarifying whether they were Loyalists or Patriots.

"Some of the regular British army officers did not respect the Loyalists, even though some Loyalist units fought well. But the command and control system of the British military was just never able to get their morale up and their men mobilized."

British military leaders believed that the capture of Savannah and Charleston would lead both Georgia and South Carolina to submit to royal authority. Local Loyalists encouraged this belief, citing enthusiastic support from a large population who remained loyal to the Crown; they would guarantee the success of a southern campaign. In late 1779, Sir Henry Clinton initiated the Southern Strategy by sending a force to seize the port of Savannah and the interior fort at Augusta. The following spring, General Clinton led one of the largest armies assembled during the Revolution to capture the major southern port of Charleston, which surrendered after enduring a siege that lasted for weeks. The British successes in Savannah, Augusta, and Charleston reinvigorated South Carolina's backcountry Loyalists. The British high command issued a call to South Carolina Loyalists to enter the King's service, and new recruits flocked to Loyalist regiments. The British offered pardons to former rebels who gave their allegiance to the Crown and, according to Clinton, "there are few men in South Carolina who are not either our prisoners or in arms with us." However, Clinton's optimism was soon tested.

Chapter 3

"They may bend, but they won't break"

When the British and their Loyalist following began to implement the Southern Strategy in the Spartan District, both Loyalists and Patriots were ready to heed the call to arms. Since 1775, the men and women in the district had debated whether or not to support the revolutionary Provincial Government in Charleston or accept continued royal authority. The choice was rarely easy, and family members often found themselves on opposing sides. Allegiances changed as well, depending largely on personal considerations rather than political conviction. During the period between late 1775 and 1780, when the British returned to claim what they believed was rightfully theirs, Patriots dominated South Carolina.

Militarily, the Spartan District was quiet until the summer of 1780, when the area exploded into outright civil war as neighbors and brothers fought each other. General Nathanael Greene, leader of the Continental Army beginning in 1780, thought the intimate nature of the fight made the war more traumatic. Loyalists and Patriots, noted Greene, "pursued each other with the most relentless fury, killing and destroying each other wherever they meet...plundering one another" and committing "private murders." Greene's characterization was evident in the South Carolina backcountry and in the Spartan District.

The Spartan Regiment, formed by John Thomas Sr. in 1775, consisted of about 200 men who had been recruited by the end of 1775. A number of them were associated with Nazareth Presbyterian Church. William Henry Drayton, one of the men who had inspired Thomas to form the regiment, arranged to supply the force with ammunition. Hoping to dilute Fletchall's influence in the area and calm dissension in the ranks, John Prince, a member of the Council of Safety, proposed to relieve Fletchall and the "obnoxious captains" in his militia unit of their military duties. Replace them, suggested Prince, with "true friends to liberty" and "immediately bring the men over." Later that year, Fletchall resigned, and men more supportive of the Patriot cause replaced "officers of doubtful allegiance." By 1777, the Patriot regiment had split into the 1st and 2nd (Upper and Lower) Spartan regiments. John Thomas commanded the 1st Spartan Regiment and Thomas Brandon commanded the 2nd, also known as the Fairforest Regiment.

During the Revolution, militia units such as the Spartan Regiment assumed great significance because the Patriots did not have a professional army until after 1777, when the Continental Army, only about 12,000 men, proved itself in battle and survived the bitter winter at Valley Forge. Until the Revolution, militia units had the main responsibility to defend the colony against the Native Americans. Militia companies consisted of 25 to 30 men who elected a captain to command them. Colonels, initially appointed by the Council of Safety, commanded regiments composed of three or more companies. They had the authority to appoint field-grade officers holding the rank of lieutenant colonel or major. Later, the new state government appointed the militia colonels and ratified their field appointments. The enlistment term was short, usually three or four weeks. Potentially, all able men in a district could be drafted into the militia. The Council of Safety, and later the General Assembly, required all colonels to prepare at least one-third of the men in each company to be "ready for instant service." Before the Battle of Cowpens in January 1781, Patriot and Loyalist militia and British Provincials, elite units of American Loyalists trained to British army standards, constituted the only military forces in the Spartan District. After the fall of Charleston and until Cowpens, the Patriot and Loyalist units in the Spartan District were all militia.

In other areas of the province, Charleston, Camden, and Ninety Six, for example, the British made use of regular army regiments or Provincial militia. Raising the Provincial troops depended on locating a man of stature to muster and arm the militia and command it. Most of the Provincial troops in South Carolina during the Revolutionary era were in DeLancey's

Brigade from New York and the New Jersey Volunteers, sent to fight in the southern campaign. The terms and conditions of their service were specified. Provincial regiments could choose their own officers and offer bounty land as an enlistment incentive. It was difficult to maintain their numbers because they did not receive the same benefits that regular British troops received. During most of the Revolutionary period, the British depended heavily on Loyalists, both Provincials and local militia units, along with a few regular British officers, to remind people that England controlled the colony.

Militia service was difficult as well as dangerous. Often, their orders required militiamen to travel great distances from home. The Spartan Regiment, for example, saw action at Ninety Six, in Cherokee country, Georgia, and near Charleston. Although militiamen were often skilled marksmen, they lacked the discipline to withstand a bayonet assault by British regulars. Once the civil war in the backcountry erupted in earnest in 1780, both Loyalist and Patriot militia had to scavenge for supplies, stealing from those whose political views were different. This behavior resulted in a number of murders and other unfortunate incidents that heightened the tense atmosphere. The return of the British to South Carolina and the collapse of Patriot resistance in the spring of 1780 ignited those tensions and passions into civil war.

FIELDS' NOTES

"Provincials drew rations. They wore uniforms and received pay. It was like a mobilized national guard. Militia training depended on the geographical area. Most of the training that a local unit received was in the use of small arms. In this part of the state, militia units were much better trained because of the ever-present Cherokee threat. By 1780, people in the Spartan District had seen a great deal of combat. The principal weapon they used was the hunting rifle, accurate for a longer range than a musket. However, it did not have a bayonet and took longer to load. Consequently, the militia had a reputation of running because they could not stand up against a British bayonet charge. If the enemy approached from 50 yards away with a bayonet, the one minute it took to reload a rifle was long enough to allow the bayonet to be utilized. So a lot of the militia criticism for running was based on just the different kind of weaponry."

When the British returned to South Carolina and occupied Charleston in May 1780, some British strategists worried that General Clinton had erred in his analysis of the temper of the backcountry. Resistance to the Crown's authority flared in the interior as rebels organized forces to oppose the occupation. Their activity was sufficient that General Clinton sent three military detachments to reestablish royal authority in the area. In May, the British occupied Camden, which became a major British supply post. Royalist officers Colonel Nisbet Balfour and Major Patrick Ferguson moved toward Ninety Six, along with Colonel Alexander Innes, commander of the South Carolina Royalists. As British forces moved into the interior, Andrew Williamson, the Patriot militia commander in the backcountry, attempted to organize a stand against the British. Upon learning that most militia officers viewed resistance as futile, Williamson abandoned his plan. A number of militia captains signed a personal parole, seemingly ceding the backcountry to England. Believing that these agreements "put an end to all resistance in South Carolina," Clinton set sail for New York, leaving Lord Cornwallis in command of the South.

Initially, Cornwallis planned to march his regular forces into North Carolina and Virginia while relying on local militia regiments to secure the southern backcountry. He appointed Major Patrick Ferguson as Inspector of Militia and ordered him to recruit Loyalist militiamen in the Ninety Six District. Brilliant and impetuous, Ferguson had proved his recruiting ability by raising a Loyalist militia in Georgia for the 1779 campaign against Savannah. The major inspired loyalty and affection among his men, making him the ideal person to recruit and train a militia force. Soon, Ferguson had at his command seven militia battalions, 4,000 men. He was certain he could field 1,500 of them on short notice to defend the frontier. Ferguson's headquarters was at Ninety Six, but in order to carry out his orders to rally the Loyalists in the backcountry, he often relied on the small forts in the Spartan District built during the Native American wars as assembly points and supply depots. The forts also offered the Loyalists the opportunity to harass, and sometimes murder, individuals in the neighborhood with Patriot sympathies. The presence of the Loyalist troops was a constant reminder of British authority to the residents of the area and thus discouraged Patriot resistance.

Some historians have described the period beginning

in mid-summer 1780 as the Second Revolution, when small-scale battles occurred in the southern states. In South Carolina, these engagements involved American Patriots versus American Loyalists, neither of whom sustained serious defeats. The results seemed insignificant at the time these actions occurred, but as a general rule, they encouraged Patriot resistance. While of relatively little importance alone, taken together, these summertime skirmishes, notably those in the Spartan District, had a profound effect on the outcome of the Revolution.

Discord returned to the Spartan District in the summer of 1780, after Charleston had fallen into British hands. It appeared that the Patriots had given up, but events proved they had not. The vicious civil war between Patriots and Loyalists that ravaged the backcountry had its origins in long-held grievances and disagreements, but until May 1780, open conflict had been held at bay. The situation changed when the British renewed efforts to subdue the backcountry by dispatching Lieutenant Colonel Banastre Tarleton to the area. Barely 23 years old, Tarleton demonstrated military skills that moved him into the highest ranks in the British army as Lieutenant Colonel of the British Legion. Tarleton was such a superb commander that Cornwallis noted "we can do no good without you." At the Waxhaws, located in modern Lancaster County near the North Carolina line, Tarleton's reputation acquired a different kind of notoriety when his men attacked a unit of Virginia Continental troops. The Patriots, who were quickly overwhelmed, presented the white flag of surrender. Rather than accept the surrender, Tarleton and his men brutally butchered or captured the entire unit. About the same time, General Clinton proclaimed that those who had taken parole, pledging not to take up arms against the King or the Loyalists, would now be required to swear allegiance to the Crown. Anyone who refused the oath would be considered an enemy. Colonel John Thomas Sr. was among many Patriots who refused to accept the new conditions.

Patriots and Loyalists in the Spartan District met in a series of battles in the summer of 1780. In many cases, a skirmish or battle aimed to avenge a previous military humiliation, an attack on civilians, or personal grievances. Small victories and the harsh treatment that British commanders imposed on the Provincial units encouraged a number of Loyalists to join the Patriots, changing the political alignment of the Spartan District. This series of battles over the course of a couple of weeks had significant consequences beyond the immediate area.

The first in the sequence of battles that took place in the Spartan District occurred in June 1780. Colonel Thomas Brandon of the Fairforest Regiment set up camp beside a deep ravine adjacent to Fairforest Creek, near what is now the town of Union. The Patriots used the camp as a base to recruit new militiamen and to confine captured Loyalists. One prisoner, Adam Steedham, escaped and alerted Captain William Cunningham, commander at a nearby Loyalist camp, who returned the next day with a small Loyalist detachment. The Loyalists surprised Brandon's men as they prepared breakfast, breaking up the camp and killing five men. Other Patriots fled and leaped into the ravine where Cunningham's mounted troops could not follow. As a result of Brandon's defeat, the Patriot movement suffered a setback. However, within a month, Brandon returned with a new set of militiamen, ready to do battle.

Brandon's defeat warned the Patriots in the Spartan District of the very real dangers posed by the British and their Loyalist allies. They were aware that much of South Carolina was in British hands. They had seen the cruelty of Tarleton and his men and recognized the fate that possibly awaited them. They were worried and discouraged. Speaking to a group of Patriot leaders, John Thomas Jr. may have articulated the stark choice confronting them. "Our cause must now be determined. Shall we join the British, or strive like men for the noble end for which we have done and spent so much? Shall we declare ourselves cowards and traitors, or shall we fight for liberty as we have life?" Joseph McJunkin, a major in the Fairforest Regiment who had survived Brandon's Defeat because he was in the woods hiding valuable powder, asked those present to "throw up their hats, clap their hands if they were committed to continued resistance to Great Britain. All responded thus." Thomas's passionate address subdued the defeatist attitudes. The new mood was one of excitement, determination, and hope.

In an attempt to further secure the Spartan District, a Loyalist captain arrested the commander of the Spartan Regiment, John Thomas Sr., and sent him to the jail at Ninety Six. The Loyalists had learned that Thomas and his family had hidden gunpowder on their property, contrary to terms of the parole he had taken after Charleston fell. Furthermore, they feared that Thomas, a well-known Patriot, might muster the old Spartan Regiment. Although Thomas spent the remainder of the war in prison, in early July, his son, John Thomas Jr., mobilized the Spartan Regiment at its muster ground near the Thomas home at Cedar Spring.

At that time, the militia colonels stored gunpowder and weapons on their personal property because there was no central regimental arsenal. Thomas Sr.'s wife, Jane, and his daughters anticipated that Loyalists might come to their home to confiscate the powder stored there. They removed the powder from the barn and hid it in the woods. Much of the gunpowder used in later battles was the powder that they had saved.

Jane Thomas took food and medicines to her husband imprisoned in the Loyalist stronghold at Ninety Six. The Loyalist jail was not a death camp, but food was in short supply, and medical care was inadequate. Often, soldiers' wives accompanied their husbands to military postings. As Mrs. Thomas stood around the campfires with other women, she listened intently to the conversation and learned that the Provincials planned to march up Blackstock Road the next day and attack a Patriot unit. Quickly, she realized they were talking about Cedar Spring and the Spartan Regiment. Before daylight, Jane Thomas, nearing age 60, left the fort at Ninety Six to ride the 60 or so miles to Cedar Spring. She arrived at some point in the afternoon, in time to warn her son and the Spartan Regiment of the planned attack that night and to foil a Loyalist ambush.

"In a British prison, the diet was meager and healthcare virtually non-existent. Prisoners' wives, sisters, and others often brought rations and medical supplies to the camps as Jane Thomas did. Back then a standard military unit, both British and American, had a certain number of positions that could be filled by soldiers' wives who actually traveled with them, the camp followers. We often think they were women of ill repute, but in most cases they were wives of the soldiers. They could even draw rations. And that is a part of both armies, because basically the women did the support work, including nursing. Back then doctors were civilians hired on contract. The nurses usually were soldiers' wives."

The Spartan Regiment camped at Cedar Spring, perhaps preparing to join Colonel Thomas Sumter's force. Sumter had resigned his commission in the Continental Army in 1778 and retired to his home. In May 1780, after British raiders burned his home, he renewed his fight against the British. He formed an army of militiamen and mounted a campaign against the British and their Loyalist allies. In the summer of 1780, the so-called Sumter's Brigade constituted the only organized force resisting British authority. In July 1780, Sumter's militia was on the northeast side of the Broad River.

Mrs. Thomas's warning gave the Patriots time to prepare for the Loyalists' arrival at Cedar Spring, near the modern-day site of the South Carolina School for the Deaf and Blind. John Thomas Jr., commander of the regiment in his father's absence, directed his 60 men to move out of sight at the rear of the camp. Blazing fires at the campsite suggested it was occupied. On the night of July 12, about 150 Loyalists attacked the camp, anticipating the destruction of the Patriot force, but the Spartan Regiment was ready for a fight. During the course of the Cedar Spring battle, some Loyalists were killed; the rest fled. Among the Loyalist casualties was John White, who had refused to fight the Native Americans in 1776 by declaring himself a non-combatant. Realizing that they might not be so lucky next time, the American Patriots moved on toward North Carolina, where they hoped to be beyond the reach of a Loyalist attack.

This first battle of Cedar Spring occurred on the same day as Huck's Defeat in York County, where a Patriot force of about 500 easily overwhelmed a Loyalist cavalry unit led by Christian Huck. Huck's Defeat was also a blow to backcountry Loyalists. The two Loyalist losses must have been disheartening and may have led Ferguson to make haste as he moved toward the area. The battle at Cedar Spring was the first Patriot challenge to Ferguson's control of the backcountry and demonstrated that the Loyalists, even under the command of a skilled officer such as Ferguson, were vulnerable. The small battle at Cedar Spring kicked off three consecutive days of fighting in the Spartan District. The story of those days is a story of brutality stemming from malicious revenge, as Patriots and Loyalists alike tried to annihilate each other.

Embarrassed by their blunder at Cedar Spring, the Loyalists made their way 20 miles north and took refuge at Gowen's Old Fort, on the South Pacolet River near the Cherokee boundary and the North Carolina line. The Loyalists held this fort and used it as a base to raid and plunder the immediate vicinity, intimidating anyone who might be a Patriot sympathizer. At the fort, the Loyalists made preparations to chase the Spartan Regiment into

North Carolina, not realizing that they were about to encounter a dangerous band of Patriots.

On July 13, a group of about 35 Georgia Patriots had abandoned their militia unit because some of the officers and many of the soldiers considered further resistance to British authority futile. Led by Colonel John Jones, they were dodging Loyalists and waiting for an opportunity to link up with a South Carolina unit to form a larger force. By pretending to be Loyalists, the Georgians secured directions to Gowen's Old Fort from local Crown sympathizers. They agreed to join the Loyalists who were pursuing the Patriots from Cedar Spring and managed to get inside the Loyalist-occupied fort on the Pacolet River near the Cherokee boundary line. After enjoying their hospitality, during the night the Georgians attacked the unsuspecting Loyalists.

In a matter of minutes the assault was over. No Patriots died in the attack, and only one Loyalist perished. The Patriots captured 35 enemy militiamen (including three who were wounded). Generously, the Patriots agreed to parole them, but destroyed most of the weapons and took the best horses with them. The victories at Cedar Spring and Gowen's Old Fort revived the spirits of the Patriots in the area who, a month earlier, had thought they were fighting an almost hopeless cause.

FIELDS' NOTES

"Every one of these frontier forts was on a major road to provide mobility so families could get there quickly. Fort Prince, for example, is on the Blackstock Road. The second need was a good water supply, usually a very bold spring. At Fort Prince, the spring still flows. They were usually near a corn mill, because in South Carolina heat, even meal does not last long. Cereal products were a significant part of the diet, and corn had to be ground frequently. Because grinding corn required water power, most forts were located near shoals and near the homes of leading families. In the 1770s, the two principal families in the northern section of the Spartan District were the Princes and the Earles, who often intermarried. Almost every one of these forts was built as a part of a Patriot or Loyalist family complex. Usually the family put a stockade around a barn so they could also use it for storage. In the event of an attack, the family and neighbors sought protection inside the stockade."

Guided by a Loyalist captive, the Georgians left Gowen's the next morning and went to Earle's Ford, a major crossing of the Pacolet River, about seven or eight miles away. There they met Colonel Charles McDowell's North Carolina militia, camped on the high ground on the east side of the North Pacolet River, about two miles from Landrum. His unit of several hundred North Carolinians had been pursuing Ferguson across the South Carolina backcountry and needed rest. Earle's Ford seemed to be a good place to camp. To be sure the area was free of Loyalists, McDowell sent out scouts on the west side of the river. When they had not returned by nightfall, McDowell mistakenly assumed that they were safe and had found a place to spend the night. The Georgians set up camp near the ford, between the North Carolina forces and the river. Thinking their position was safe, all the Patriots rested.

Unfortunately, the scouts were not safe; they could not report back to McDowell because they were lost. McDowell's assumption left his men and the Georgians open to attack. After learning of the events at Gowen's Old Fort, a force of about 70 Loyalist dragoons, or mounted soldiers, commanded by Major James Dunlap, a British officer, moved up from Fort Prince to retaliate. Fort

Prince, located on the Blackstock Road, very close to the North and South Carolina line, pre-dated the American Revolution. Like other backcountry forts nearby, Fort Prince had protected the people of the area during the Native American raids in the 1750s. One of the most important British posts in the backcountry, it was a circular structure built of heavy timbers, 12 to 15 feet high. A ditch surrounding the fort provided additional security and afforded a good defensive position. The cleared land around the fort created excellent sight lines for marksmen inside. After driving a Patriot force out of Fort Prince, British Provincials, commanded by Colonel Alexander Innes, an officer in the regular army, occupied the fort in the summer of 1780.

The Loyalist dragoons slipped quietly across the river after dark on July 14, and, using bayonets and knives, butchered several of the sleeping Georgia militiamen at Earle's Ford. The rest of the Georgians withdrew to McDowell's camp, and the combined force fought and pushed the Loyalists back across the river. Dunlap and his men had expected to attack 30 Patriots, but instead met a force of several hundred. Eight Patriots, most of them Georgians, died in the battle at Earle's Ford. Dunlap's outnumbered men retreated to the Bayliss Earle home across the river.

The next morning, July 15, the surviving Georgians asked Colonel McDowell to give them a force and supplies sufficient to attack the Provincials. Before sunrise, 52 Patriot horsemen were in hot pursuit of the Loyalists. The ensuing battle lasted all day, as the opposing sides ranged 20 miles down the Blackstock Road to Fort Prince. During that day, the most noteworthy skirmish occurred about noon on Lawson's Fork, near present-day Inman, where the Patriots surprised the Loyalists, and killed eight of them. The rest, despite Major Dunlap's effort to keep order, scattered and retreated toward Fort Prince.

The Patriots, who had advanced to within 300 yards of Fort Prince, backed off, realizing that a successful attack was impossible. Occupied by more than 300 Loyalists, the fort was well fortified and well supplied. Without cannon, breaching the fort's walls would be impossible, so the Patriot force withdrew toward Earle's Ford. Major Ferguson, fearing a larger Patriot force would return and attack the fort, ordered an evacuation to his headquarters camp on Fairforest Creek near Union.

Patriots and Loyalists had fought four battles in four days with a minimal loss of lives. As a result, by the end of July, the British and their Loyalist supporters had withdrawn from their principal stronghold in the Spartan District; Fort Thicketty was the last Loyalist bastion in the upper reaches of the Spartan District. The Patriots clearly had the momentum. Word traveled quickly in the backcountry, and many Patriots who thought the cause was lost saw a glimmer of hope. Loyalists worried.

After the Loyalists evacuated Fort Prince, the tenor of the conflict in the Spartan District changed. Thus far the struggle had been waged almost entirely by local militia, but at the end of July 1780, Patriot militia from other states arrived in the area to join the fight. The next campaign involved forces moving in from neighboring states to fight in the area. Elijah Clark led a large force in from Georgia. Though not a South Carolina native, Clark had lived for several years near Grindal Shoals when he was a young man. Later, he moved to the Georgia frontier, near the Savannah River. In 1774, he supported the King, but, like so many other Patriot militiamen, he joined the other side once fighting had begun. Experienced as a Native American fighter, Lieutenant Colonel Clark had led his militia force to victory over a Loyalist detachment at Kettle Creek in 1779. He brought his forces to South Carolina to fight with his cousins and other kinsmen. The Overmountain Men, militia units commanded by Isaac Shelby, arrived from across the mountains of what is now North Carolina and Tennessee. Shelby, still a young man in his 20s, had served the Patriot cause in various ways before being appointed militia colonel by the North Carolina governor. These various military commands began to network into a force large enough to win larger battles, and to defend the area against Ferguson's Loyalist army of about 1,500 men.

"Patrick Ferguson was renowned as possibly the best living marksman and was more than willing to show off his skill. A career soldier, he had invented a breech-loading rifle that could be reloaded quickly and fired with more accuracy than other weapons in use at the time. Ferguson was a much better officer than Banastre Tarleton. If Tarleton had been killed at Kings Mountain instead of Ferguson, the end of the story might have been different because Ferguson knew how to motivate and train men. And he took these local Loyalist units and transformed them into a powerful military force."

Fort Thicketty, also known as Anderson's Fort, was near the Pacolet River in the eastern section of the Spartan District, now Cherokee County. The location was another ideal spot from which the Loyalists could launch raids on Patriot farms, terrifying the people and ensuring that they would accept British authority. The fort was much stouter than some of the other forts in the area that had often been hastily erected in the face of Native American attacks. A strong abatis of tree branches protruding from the walls surrounded the circular structure. The sole entrance was a tunnel through the abatis, with barely enough space for one man to crawl through. Many considered Fort Thicketty impregnable.

Folks in the area were well acquainted with the marauding activities of the fort's garrison. The Loyalists had attacked a number of Patriots, stolen their belongings, and threatened the women who were often alone while the men were away fighting. When a Loyalist band stole her family's clothes and bed linens, Jane McJunkin chased after a mounted rider who had taken her quilt and tried to pull it off the horse and out of his hands. Laughing, the Loyalists said she could keep the quilt if she could get it away from the man who held the other end. A good outcome for McJunkin seemed unlikely, until the Loyalist's horse slipped, throwing the rider, and giving her an opportunity to yank the quilt out of his hands. She put her foot on his chest and pulled the quilt from him.

The Spartan District, located between Georgia and North Carolina, was strategically important to both the American Patriots and the British. On July 30, a contingent composed of several militia units from three states moved toward Fort Thicketty, intending to eliminate the last major

Loyalist presence in the area. Charles McDowell and Isaac Shelby were from North Carolina. Elijah Clark came from Georgia, and the Spartan Regiment under Captain Josiah Culbertson joined them. The combined force consisted of about 600 men, a significant number of them North Carolinians under Colonel Shelby. Ferguson, whose main camp was on Fairforest Creek south of present-day Union, ordered Patrick Moore, the commander, to hold Fort Thicketty as long as possible. Moore initially refused to obey the Patriots' demand that the fort surrender, acceding to the wishes of his men. The Patriots then moved in "fake cannon," logs mounted on wheels, the end facing the fort marked with a black circle. The Patriots pretended to load and prepare to fire. Fooled by the Patriot performance, Moore left the protection of the fort to speak with the Patriots and surrendered. Without firing a shot, the Patriots acquired more than 200 weapons, along with a supply of powder and shot at Fort Thicketty. Shelby, in charge of the expedition, paroled the 93 prisoners, and the Patriots moved toward McDowell's camp at Cherokee Ford on the Savannah River.

The surrender of Fort Thicketty was a coup for the Patriots, especially in light of the events of the previous month. The unanticipated Patriot successes threw Ferguson off balance and a wrench into the Loyalist battle plans. After the surrender of Fort Thicketty, Clark and Shelby continued their pursuit of Ferguson and his Loyalist militia, keeping on the move to elude discovery while Ferguson tried to surprise them.

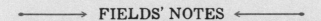

FIELDS' NOTES

"Sometimes battles are named for the nearest cultural center, and the nearest there was Cedar Spring. Others called it the Battle of Wofford's Ironworks because that is where the battle ended. That battle took place along what was then called the Great Wagon Road. We call it now the Old Georgia Road. That was the third of the great wagon roads through South Carolina. The first was through Camden to Augusta. The second one follows South Carolina 121 through Rock Hill and on to Augusta. The Old Georgia Road started in Charlotte like the other two and went through this area into north Georgia. The Georgia Road and the Blackstock Road were the major roads. Most of the major battles fought in late July and August occurred near them."

Although the Patriot force numbered about a thousand men, it rarely operated as a single unit. Instead, the commanders dispatched smaller groups to various areas with a specific mission, a plan that had certain advantages. A smaller guerrilla group was easier for officers to control, because it could move more rapidly to an objective and could secure adequate supplies of food and fodder. Colonel McDowell sent Colonels Isaac Shelby and Elijah Clark and their men to track Ferguson as his men ranged through the backcountry. The Patriots learned that Ferguson had been recruiting in the area of Fairforest Creek, coercing men to join his unit, even if they had accepted parole and promised not to aid the Crown. The Loyalists reportedly stopped along the way as they moved through the backcountry, scavenging for food and often finding hospitality at the homes of local Loyalists.

On August 7, 1780, the Patriots halted at a crossroads on the Georgia Road between Cedar Spring and Wofford's Ironworks in the Spartan District. Josiah Culbertson, one of Shelby's men who lived nearby, received permission to visit his home. En route, he stumbled upon the Loyalists and calmly rode through their camp as if he belonged there, taking note of every detail. From Culbertson, Shelby and Clark learned that Ferguson was only a half-mile away, and the Patriot commanders led 600 mounted militia to engage him. The ensuing battle, known as Second Cedar Spring, Battle of the Peach Trees, or Wofford's Ironworks, began at daylight near Fairforest Creek and moved east along the Georgia Road, past Cedar Spring, and ended late in the day at the ironworks on Lawson's Fork.

The Patriots broke camp and set up a defensive position along Fairforest Creek on the Georgia Road. Ferguson dispatched Major James Dunlap and a force consisting of several dozen dragoons and mounted militia to attack the Patriot camp. The outnumbered Patriots were forced to retreat up the Georgia Road, but fought delaying skirmishes to give themselves time to amass a force large enough to fight. In the hand-to-hand fighting, Patriots were forced to withdraw, engaging the Loyalists along the way. The call went out throughout the area, summoning Patriot militiamen to meet at the crossroads (where present-day Dogwood Club Road intersects with Old Petrie Road) at noon. Several hundred responded. About noon, the fighting intensified, and the Patriots pushed the Loyalists along the Georgia Road until Ferguson arrived with reinforcements, increasing the size of the Loyalist contingent to 1,200 men. Patriot leaders knew better than to risk a pitched battle with a superior force, so they retreated toward the ironworks and the Pacolet River, fighting skirmishing actions all the way. Near the present-day Oak Forest Plantation neighborhood, where the Georgia Road crosses Three Mile Branch, the Patriots held the Loyalists long enough to set up a defensive position at dusk on the high ground across Lawson's Fork near the ironworks. Ferguson, cognizant of the strength of the Patriot defenses, chose not to attack in spite of the taunts and jeers delivered by the Patriots to goad the Loyalists into a confrontation. Ferguson decided to wait until the next day to make a daylight assault. The Patriots built up fires to simulate a camp as they pulled out across the river late that night. Withdrawing was not an admission of defeat but a tactic to save the Patriot force from total destruction.

For Ferguson and the Loyalists, the day-long battle along the Georgia Road was a hollow victory that had presented an opportunity for Ferguson to regain control of a sizeable area in the backcountry. The Patriots, however, were heartened by the day's actions. For the first time, a combined Patriot militia large enough to engage in face-to-face combat with the enemy had shown courage and steadfastness in the face of enemy fire. The number of casualties is disputed, but it appears that Loyalist losses far outweighed those of the Patriots, who may have lost as few as a dozen men.

→ FIELDS' NOTES ←

"Basically the Patriots based their strategy on mobility. Most militiamen went to a battle on a horse. Commanders did not like that much because a horse would eat more than a man and they could not feed horses for several days. They did not want the horses there until they were needed. With fast horses, they could mobilize very quickly, get to a place and fight, and if necessary, retreat quickly before they were destroyed. They never wanted to lose an army. Lose a battle, but do not lose your army. Militiamen learned how to defend themselves and turn the rifle into an offensive weapon against the British bayonet and musket. The European strategy was: All line up, mass fire. The Patriots knew they could never defeat the British using that tactic. So they began to develop new strategies and tactics based on using the horse, the rifle, and local weapons like tomahawks and knives instead of bayonets. The Patriots learned those tactics from the Cherokees."

About a week after Shelby and Clark abandoned their position at Wofford's Ironworks, a Patriot army composed of both Continental troops and militia suffered a humiliating defeat near the important transportation hub of Camden. The American hero of Saratoga, General Horatio Gates, ordered an attack on Lord Cornwallis's army. With a force that outnumbered the British two to one, Gates should have had the upper hand. However, his tactical plan was poorly conceived and imperfectly executed. In the face of a determined British advance, the Patriots, unlike those at the Battle of the Peach Orchard, threw down their weapons and ran. At Camden, the main Patriot army in the South was decimated in about an hour. As many as one-third of the Patriot force died in the battle. Another third became prisoners of the British. The rest scattered and fled, most eventually making their way to North Carolina. This disaster at Camden cost General Gates his command. When the American Congress appointed General Nathanael Greene to succeed him, Patriot fortunes began to improve. The Patriot defeat at Camden was followed two days later by an equally disastrous and humiliating rout at Fishing Creek. There, 350 Loyalists led by Banastre Tarleton took a Patriot camp by complete surprise. The Patriot commander, Thomas Sumter, lost 150 men and saw 300 of his men wounded or captured, along with a few Continentals. The victors freed 100 British prisoners. Only 16 Loyalists died. However, a battle on August 19 at Musgrove Mill had a different outcome.

Musgrove Mill was on the Enoree River in Laurens County, just beyond the Spartanburg County line. Edward Musgrove, an educated man born in England, was well known in the area for his grist mill and for his legal expertise. Too old to join in the fray, Musgrove nonetheless sympathized with the Loyalists, but reportedly asked God in his nightly prayers to return peace and harmony to the area. During the bloody summer of 1780, the British found Musgrove's property, with its ford to facilitate transportation and grist mill to provide food, was an ideal site for a supply post and hospital camp where the wounded from previous battles in July and August could receive care. About 200 people were at the camp, most of them supply and hospital workers. Few trained military personnel were at the camp.

After the brutal day along the Georgia Road, the Patriots linked up with Colonel Charles McDowell and his North Carolina militia who were camping in the Spartan District, across the Broad River at Head's Ford. While in camp, three Patriot colonels—James Williams from South Carolina, Elijah Clark from Georgia, and Isaac Shelby from Tennessee—designed a coordinated attack on Musgrove Mill. Shelby and Clark had previously led a combined command; James Williams was a newcomer. A wealthy and well-known figure in the vicinity of Musgrove Mill, Williams had served under Colonel Thomas Sumter, with whom he had a falling out. The three colonels secured powder and supplies from the North Carolina regiment. To motivate their men, they spread a rumor that the British held cash for the payroll at the Musgrove Mill camp. In those days, money was scarce, forcing the people to trade and barter in exchange for goods and services. Consequently, the possibility of acquiring a military payroll of British coins was quite alluring. Whether there was a British payroll at Musgrove Mill or not, the prospect of one might have motivated the militiamen.

"The Patriots were learning to network into a powerful military force. It was based on the horse, on mobility, on tomahawks and knives. The leaders, rather than the common soldiers, were the ones who were learning. The common soldiers also changed as the war progressed, and by the summer of 1780, they began to trust their leaders enough to do risky things. Musgrove Mill was one of the first offensive battles. Up to that point, almost all summer, the battles and skirmishes were defensive. At Musgrove Mill, the Patriots turned to offense with a very risky operation. It was what is now called a raid in force, moving in quickly with a limited mission and then moving out quickly. Musgrove Mill was probably the only Revolutionary War battle that was run by a committee. The three commanders never agreed on who would be the overall commander. Some say Williams was, because he was the local person, and he had the center position of the three regiments, straddling the road, but there is no documentation to show that."

A mounted force of about 200 Patriots rode 45 miles, planning to go behind the British line. Cornwallis had ordered Ferguson to move his Loyalists across the Broad River in order to protect his flank at Camden. Most of the Provincials had also moved across the river. The Patriots circled around Ferguson's camp on Fairforest Creek quietly at night and arrived at Musgrove Mill well before daylight. They sent out a patrol, and when the scouts returned, the Patriots learned two things. The South Carolina Royalists, a Provincial unit from what is now the Greenwood area, reinforced by British Provincials from New York and New Jersey, had arrived at Musgrove Mill the day before. Instead of facing 200 largely untrained local militia, the Patriots faced a trained force numbering between 500 and 600. In addition, the Patriot scouts had encountered a Loyalist patrol on the outskirts of the camp, robbing the Patriots of the element of surprise. The Patriot commanders had to make a decision. A direct attack was imprudent because of the superior military force now at the camp. Retreat was virtually impossible because the horses were worn out, and the Loyalists would likely overtake the Patriots on the road and decimate the force.

Seeing no other option, the Patriots constructed a hewn log and brush semi-circular fortification on the ridge overlooking the Enoree River. Captain Shadrack Inman, a Georgian, volunteered to lead a group of 16 volunteers across the river towards the Loyalist camp and to fire as if they were attacking. Their arrival roused the camp, creating disruption and confusion. The Loyalists took the bait and followed the retreating Patriots across the Enoree River, straight into an ambush. The Patriot fortification created a "killing field," and when the Loyalists entered it, the Patriots gave them devastating fire and then assaulted them in hand-to-hand combat. Brandishing tomahawks and axes, and shrieking something like a Cherokee war cry, the Patriots chased the Provincials the half mile or so to the river. When the Loyalist force began to disintegrate and the men began to run away, one Loyalist was not too tired to "turn up his buttock in derision at the Americans." A Patriot promptly shot him.

The Loyalist troops, even though trained and experienced, blundered in fleeing, one of the worse reactions for a military unit because order and discipline are lost. Loyalist casualties in that hour-long battle, including killed, wounded, and captured, was larger than the entire Patriot force. Among those wounded was Captain Alexander Innes, who had commanded the Loyalist Provincials. Only 10 Patriots perished, including Captain Shadrack Inman. The casualty ratio between the two forces makes the Battle of Musgrove Mill one of the most successful Patriot victories of the Revolution.

The battle at Musgrove Mill marks the first time the Patriots had gone on the offensive; the earlier battles were defensive. For a month, the Patriot militia had kept Ferguson at bay, all the while honing their military skills and building up their confidence. The action at Musgrove Mill proved the Patriots had learned to damage the British without destroying themselves. The militia colonels and captains had learned how to cooperate and build brigade-size units. The three Patriot colonels—Williams, Clark, and Shelby—agreed if they could cooperate and defeat the Loyalists at Musgrove Mill, with a bigger force they could defeat Ferguson. They proved the accuracy of their idea at Kings Mountain early in October 1780.

Although the Patriots considered marching on the Loyalist stronghold at Ninety Six, when they learned of the Patriot rout at Camden, they decided to head towards the mountains, embarking on an exhausting 70-mile, non-stop, circuitous journey to North Carolina. En route, the Patriots sustained themselves with the peaches and green corn in the fields they passed.

The commanders realized that they were the only Patriot force still operating in the backcountry. Shelby and the Overmountain Men, whose enlistment term was about to end, marched home across the mountains. Most of the rest of the Patriot militia also headed toward home. Williams escorted the 70 prisoners from Musgrove Mill to Gates's headquarters in Hillsboro, North Carolina. For his leadership during the battle, Williams was named a brigadier general. Colonels Clark and Shelby agreed to continue scouting Ferguson and to keep each other apprised of his whereabouts. With the last remaining Patriot militia now across the state line in North Carolina, British officials thought the South Carolina backcountry was finally pacified. They were mistaken.

General Horatio Gates had fled Camden before the battle had even ended, landing in Hillsboro, North Carolina. As many as 700 of his men eventually joined him as he prepared to regroup. Colonel Thomas Sumter, seeking to redeem himself after the humiliating defeat at Fishing Creek, had mustered a force of 1,000 militiamen, as General Gates ordered, to harass Ferguson. Cornwallis, thinking that controlling North Carolina was the key to dominating its southern neighbor, moved his British regulars up to Charlotte.

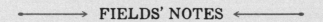 **FIELDS' NOTES**

"James Williams had been with Thomas Sumter's regiment until the two had a falling out and Williams joined other forces. Williams was a highly structured man, a Presbyterian elder and rather wealthy. He did not get along well with Sumter. Some believe Williams took too much credit for the victory at Musgrove Mill. Afterwards, General Gates persuaded the South Carolina governor to appoint Williams brigadier general, a move that irritated Sumter. There was a lot of bad feeling among the South Carolina leadership between Sumter's colonels who were loyal to him and the militia units in this area. Williams was shot and killed near the end of the battle of Kings Mountain and afterwards, Sumter's colonels maligned him for the rest of the war.

"The circumstances of Williams's death are still unknown. Some say he died as a result of friendly fire, because there was such resentment against him. Probably the best case scenario is that there was chaos at the top of that mountain, and Williams died as the Patriots were getting control. He could have died as a result of friendly fire, but not necessarily vengeance fire."

Beginning in September 1780, Major Patrick Ferguson undertook to prevent Colonels McDowell and Clark from combining their forces as they had so successfully at Musgrove Mill. The British officer's aim was to protect Ninety Six and provide his men, many of them new recruits, an opportunity to test their military mettle. Many of Ferguson's men were in the Loyalist regiments raised in the Spartan District, commanded by Daniel Plummer and Zacharias Gibbes. When Ferguson pledged to "hang your leaders and lay waste to your country with fire and sword," Isaac Shelby mustered the Overmountain Men on September 25 at Sycamore Shoals on the Watauga River near Elizabethton, Tennessee. Perhaps 1,000 answered the call, prepared to fight for the Patriot cause. The Overmountain Men headed in the direction of Charlotte; en route they met Clark and Williams and their militiamen. They set up camp in the northern section of the Spartan District, and soon Sumter and his militia joined them. Patriot spies informed the militias that Ferguson had been ordered to join Cornwallis's main army at Charlotte. The combined Patriot forces marched off in pursuit of Ferguson, who was confident that he could defeat the Patriots. The British major took up a defensive position at Kings Mountain.

Major James Dunlap, leader of the Loyalist militia at both Earle's Ford and Wofford's Ironworks, did not accompany Ferguson to Kings Mountain because he was recovering from an injury sustained in North Carolina. The cruel behavior of Dunlap, a member of the Queen's Rangers, had aroused the wrath of many in the South Carolina backcountry. Several men from the Spartan District learned of Dunlap's whereabouts and went to Gilbert Town, near present-day Rutherfordton, North Carolina, to find him. They blamed him for the deaths of several of their friends earlier in the summer and planned to kill him. When they located Dunlap, the Spartans shot him as he lay in bed, and made a quick getaway. Legend and family histories suggest that Dunlap died that day in September, but it is clear that he survived and died from wounds incurred in a fight with Patriots at Ninety Six about six months later.

Ferguson had no fear of Patriot militia, so he did not bother to set up a defensive line. The Patriot commanders devised a simple plan to attack three sides of the mountain at one time. The assault began late in the afternoon of October 7, 1780. British bayonets and artillery proved useless on the mountainsides. Using guerrilla tactics, the Patriots fired at the Loyalists from cover created by the mountain's natural vegetation. Ferguson comported himself as expected of a British officer, but the valiant effort to rally his men during the battle ended with his death. The Patriots were in no mood to give quarter to the vanquished.

When the remainder of Ferguson's force surrendered, numbering nearly 700, the victorious Patriots exacted their revenge for Tarleton's cruelty, Dunbar's meanness, and other outrageous actions against Patriots. On the victory march, Patriots plundered farms of Loyalists, but also of Patriots. They withheld food and water from their captives. Colonel Thomas Brandon of the Fairforest Regiment discovered one of the Loyalist captives hiding in a tree hollow, jerked him from the hiding place, and cut him into pieces. Stressed and exhilarated from the battle and their triumph, Patriots, such as Brandon, found ways to avenge the injuries imposed by the Loyalists on their friends and family.

The Patriots were jubilant. They had soundly trounced an army of about 900 Provincials while losing only 28 killed and 62 wounded. With Cornwallis less than a day's ride away, the Overmountain Men returned home. The South and North Carolina militiamen organized a trial of some of the Loyalists at the plantation known as Bickerstaff's Old Fields, not far from Kings Mountain. They justified their action as retaliation for Patriot prisoners who had been hanged by the British at Camden and Ninety Six. Of the 36 Loyalists condemned to death that day at Bickerstaff's, nine were hanged. The stunning blow to the British ambitions at Kings

Mountain gave a new turn to the war, forcing Cornwallis to leave Charlotte and return to South Carolina so he could protect Camden, Ninety Six, and Augusta.

Ferguson's death dictated a change in Cornwallis's plan. He still needed to establish a strong British presence in the South Carolina backcountry. Banastre Tarleton was chasing Francis Marion, the Swamp Fox, in the swamps near the coast, so Cornwallis dispatched Major James Wemyss to attack Sumter's force, surprising them at their camp on the Broad River at Fish Dam Ford near present-day Chester. In addition, he ordered a band of assassins to target Sumter. Wemyss intended to surprise Sumter, but scouts sent on patrol by the Patriot leader alerted him to the British presence. The attack failed, as did the plan to assassinate Sumter. Wemyss, who was captured after the battle, had a detailed list of Patriots he had executed and homesteads he had destroyed. The list would have enraged the Patriot army, so Sumter threw it in the fire.

In August, in the midst of the battles in the Spartan District, General Cornwallis had observed that the British were in "a civil war; there is no admitting of neutral characters & those who are not clearly with us must be so far considered against us …[and] every measure taken to prevent their being able to do mischief." Throughout South Carolina, Patriots had been harassing both the British troops and local Loyalists at every opportunity. Exasperated at the Crown's inability to maintain order, Cornwallis determined to dispatch Banastre Tarleton, perhaps his most capable officer, to the backcountry to complete the job of recruiting Loyalists that Ferguson had started. Tarleton's previous forays into the backcountry had generated fear and hatred among the settlers, both Patriots and Loyalists. The memory of his behavior at the battle of Waxhaws, where the British continued to shoot Patriots who had tendered their surrender, was still fresh. This so-called Tarleton's Quarter became a rallying cry in the backcountry, yet another example of Tarleton's brutality. The people of the backcountry dreaded his return.

Eleven days after the British failure at Fish Dam Ford, on November 20, 1780, Sumter's army encountered Tarleton at the Battle of Blackstock's. Thomas Sumter, newly commissioned brigadier general, chose an advantageous place to make a stand—Blackstock's farm, just south of the Tyger River, near Cross Anchor in Union County. Mary Blackstock, whose husband was in Colonel Benjamin Roebuck's regiment of Sumter's militia, emphatically told

Sumter that she would "not have any fighting around my house," but the stage was already set for a confrontation.

Tarleton planned to trap the Patriots in camp behind enemy lines at Fort Williams, near Clinton. His army moved up the Enoree River to take control of the fords and prevent Sumter from escaping to North Carolina. He thought the Patriots would be caught between the strong British garrison at Ninety Six and the Enoree River. Warned of Tarleton's plan by a Loyalist deserter, Sumter altered course. Colonel Brandon advised Sumter of the defensive advantages at Blackstock's Plantation, on the south side of the Tyger River. The site was on the Blackstock Road where it crossed the Tyger River at a well-known ford. Sumter's army raced to the Enoree River, managing to cross just ahead of Tarleton's army, and then rushed to Blackstock's Plantation, arriving on November 20. Patriots continued to arrive throughout the afternoon, numbering a thousand by nightfall. Noticing that Tarleton had left his slow-moving infantry and artillery and ordered his mounted dragoons on a forced march towards Sumter, Mary Dillard rode her horse around the British army and alerted the Patriots.

The rugged terrain provided defensive advantages. Sumter spread the militia units along the ridges and at

Blackstock Road where it runs between two hills to block the British approach. Tarleton refused to attack the strong Patriot defensive works, so Sumter ordered an attack to force the battle. As the British proceeded up the hill, the Patriots under Colonel Henry Hampton delivered scathing fire. The next maneuver, a cavalry charge at the road led by Tarleton, resulted in terrible casualties for his British regulars. Later, eyewitnesses reported that the road was full of dead and wounded men and horses.

When the battle seemed to be winding down, General Sumter rode to an advanced observation post. Members of a British platoon turned and fired at him. Sumter, seriously wounded in his shoulder and spine, left the field of battle to his next senior officer. Tarleton retreated two miles from the battlefield to wait for his infantry to arrive. The Patriots thought that further fighting at this location was dangerous as Tarleton moved forward with his cannon. Ever mindful that Cornwallis and his larger army were at Winnsboro, the major Patriot force abandoned Blackstock's. However, a covering force left behind kept the campfires burning all night as the Patriots slipped across the Tyger River and dispersed.

The British losses at Blackstock's were staggering. Tarleton, seeking to minimize the scope of his defeat, reported only 51 killed in his report to Cornwallis, but other sources report the total number killed was 92, with 100 wounded. The Patriots reported three killed and four wounded. While the battle did not reach a decisive conclusion, the Patriots considered Blackstock's battle a victory. They had fought the best of the British troops and inflicted severe losses. Patriot commanders kept their force intact and moved out during the night to go home and prepare to fight again.

The Battle at Blackstock's marks the first time during the American Revolutionary War that an all-militia Patriot force defeated a force of all British regulars. Tarleton's defeat at Blackstock's destroyed his reputation of invincibility. The defeat of the most hated and feared British officer lifted the spirits of the Patriots and alarmed the Loyalists. The battle showed a new sophistication in the way Patriot officers used their meager resources and knowledge of the terrain to the best advantage. Blackstock's was an example of a mobile defense in which a commander uses his forces to attack vigorously on portions of the field while guiding the enemy to attack his strongest defenses. During the two-hour battle, the British army lost more than half the number who later died at Yorktown during a three-week siege.

The small battles and skirmishes during the summer and fall of 1780 in the Spartan District led up to Kings Mountain. The Battle at Blackstock's prepared the way for General Greene to send General Morgan into the area and turn the tide at Cowpens. The British defeat there, according to General Henry Clinton, was one of "the worst consequences to the King's affairs in South Carolina, and unhappily the first link in a chain of evils that followed in regular succession until they at last ended in the loss of America."

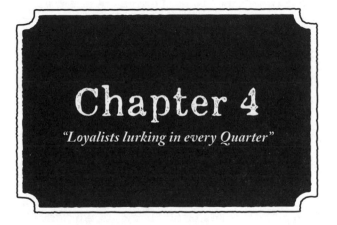

Chapter 4

"Loyalists lurking in every Quarter"

Clashes between Patriots and Loyalists had been raging in the Spartan District since 1775 when many settlers chose whether or not to support British authority. The summer and fall months of 1780 represented the high point of Loyalist participation in the war in the backcountry. Soon Loyalist support eroded, and most people allied with the Patriots or remained uncommitted. By the end of 1780, the Native Americans had been driven out of the area, and the stage had been set for ending British rule in South Carolina. However, the animosity between Patriots and Loyalists grew stronger after the final exchange of volleys at Blackstock's, and the civil war of the Revolutionary period became more intense in the Spartan District. Patriots and Loyalists engaged in vicious reprisals against each other, seeking vengeance for acts of cruelty that had occurred since 1775, when South Carolina first found itself bitterly divided.

Six weeks before the battle at Blackstock's, General Nathanael Greene, a Quaker from Rhode Island, arrived in North Carolina to assume command of the Continental Army in the South. He replaced General Horatio Gates, whose disastrous defeat at Camden might have ended the Patriot dream of independence. The presence of Greene and his experienced Continental troops in the backcountry changed the character of the war in the region and led to the final battle in the Spartan District.

Upon reaching Charlotte in December 1780, Greene found the southern army demoralized, hungry, and short of ammunition and supplies. Without a force strong enough to engage General Cornwallis in a set-piece battle, Greene violated a cardinal precept of military command by dividing his army despite the superior strength of Cornwallis's force. He dispatched General Daniel Morgan to the area west of the Broad River in South Carolina—the Spartan District.

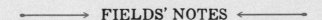 **FIELDS' NOTES**

"Morgan called the men he fought with the 'old swords.' He was an unusual person. A person like Morgan is almost like a miracle. Where did a person like that come from? Off the frontier with no formal education and able to achieve what he achieved. He showed up in Winchester, Virginia, at the age of 16 after he had a falling out with his father. Three states claim that he was born there. More than likely, he was born in New Jersey. After moving to Virginia, he never talked to his family again and never talked about them to anybody. His life started in Winchester. He was a frontiersman, a giant, strong physically. He was a brawler and won several championships, fighting with no rules.

"He joined the militia during the French and Indian War as a wagoner. He worked for somebody else as a wagoner. Then he bought his own wagon and became a contractor, hauling supplies for the British in the French and Indian War. A British officer whipped him, some say 500 lashes. They meant to kill him, but he always said 'they didn't give me but 499 lashes; they owe me one.' He joked about that.

His wife Abigail Bailey had some education, and she taught him how to read and write. She pushed him to learn arithmetic, mathematics. He must have had a brilliant mind at that age to start off with reading and writing. He probably could count, but he didn't know much more.

"He was a hard worker, a very aggressive

> businessman. And other businessmen in the area took an interest in him and went into business with him, including a Quaker iron maker. For about ten years before the Revolution, he lived as a successful farmer."

Once he had determined the lay of the land, Morgan suggested an attack on Ninety Six, the major British outpost in the backcountry, but Greene cautioned against such a strategy. Instead, Morgan's orders called for disrupting British supply lines and spiriting up the people, a task at which he proved particularly adept. Meanwhile, Cornwallis, worried about the safety of the British post at Ninety Six, sent Lieutenant Colonel Banastre Tarleton and 1,150 dragoons, infantry, and artillery from Winnsboro across the Broad River into the Spartan District. Tarleton's ultimate purpose was to crush South Carolina Patriot resistance and free Cornwallis to strike in North Carolina and then march towards Virginia. He planned to stop Morgan and his men at the Broad River, trapping them between Cornwallis's larger army and his smaller dragoon unit.

"Under state law, militia colonels could mobilize a company for 30 days against their will and move them for 30 days, the maximum that a unit could be required to be away from home. A commander had to learn how to motivate his people so they would do things that were not legally required. General Daniel Morgan at Cowpens had militia units from Virginia who had signed a contract with the state to be gone for 90 days. Their time was expiring, and Morgan had to convince them to wait a few more days so they could fight at Cowpens. You see a classic example of motivation in Morgan. He went to that campfire every night and showed his back where the British had given him lashes. He still carried the scars. He was showing these frontier men 'I'm a frontier man like you. I'm tough. I know your needs. I'm going to watch out for you. We have to get this plan together so we can defeat Tarleton.'"

Reaching the Spartan District on December 21, 1780, Morgan established his camp on the Pacolet River at Grindal Shoals, a major crossroads that allowed his men to move quickly in any direction. Upon learning of their arrival, local volunteer militiamen gathered to augment the Continental troops, including the Spartan Regiment, which formed a vital segment of Morgan's force. The Long Cane militia commanded by Colonel Andrew Pickens joined them. Pickens, who had fought in the Native American wars and with Elijah Clark at Kettle Creek, had joined other Patriot militia commanders in taking parole after the fall of Charleston and Ninety Six in May 1780. His heart, however, was with the Patriot cause. After the Loyalists destroyed his property and frightened his family, Pickens broke his parole, mustered his militia, and arrived at Grindal Shoals with about a hundred men. He knew that if he was captured, he would be hanged. Pickens had overall command of the combined militia forces at Cowpens.

Morgan's force camped at Grindal Shoals for nearly three weeks before Tarleton located them. His discovery set in motion a chase through the Spartan District that compelled the Patriots to make a new camp at Burr's Mill on Thicketty Creek and culminated in a decisive engagement at

Hannah's Cowpens, now the Cowpens National Battlefield, near the North Carolina line.

The guerrilla nature of the war in the backcountry assured that soldiers on both sides would come in contact with civilians whose help often proved useful. The danger to civilians was all too real in the intense partisanship that characterized war in the Spartan District. Anne Kennedy, a comely young Patriot woman, lived near the Broad River. According to legend, with a pistol hidden in her bosom, she rode alone to request that Morgan send men to stop Loyalists from terrorizing the locals. En route, Kennedy had several near encounters with Loyalist bands, but she managed to get through to the Patriot camp. Later, Kennedy watched Tarleton's army pass her home and rode once again to Morgan's camp to alert him of the size and composition of the British forces. On other occasions, Kennedy carried messages to the Patriots, hiding them in her stockings.

The story of Kate Barry, daughter of Charles and Mary Moore who lived at Walnut Grove Plantation, is well known in the Spartan District. Barry, a young mother and a Patriot, reportedly tied her child to a bedpost at her home and took off on her horse to warn her husband, a captain in the Spartan Regiment, that the British were approaching.

Captain Andrew Barry's men reached the Patriot camp just before the Battle of Cowpens. According to tradition, Barry also carried messages, spied on the enemy, and rallied folks to join the Patriot effort during January 1781.

With Tarleton nearer than expected, about daylight on January 16, 1781, Morgan and his men beat a hasty retreat from the new camp on Thicketty Creek, leaving behind the remnants of their breakfast. Cognizant of the superior training and experience of Tarleton's force and his personal grudge against the Patriots of the area after Blackstock's, Morgan selected a strategically suitable spot for establishing a defensive position—the pasture and crossroads known locally as Hannah's Cowpens. The Patriots reached the Cowpens during the afternoon on a cold day, January 16, 1781, and set up camp in one of the swales or depressions that dotted the area. Dozens of backcountry militiamen, familiar with Hannah's Cowpens, joined them, arriving even as the battle commenced the next morning. About 1,400 to 1,600 Patriots, Continentals and militia made up Morgan's army, a change from earlier battles in the district fought solely by local militia.

Expecting Tarleton to make an aggressive frontal assault, his customary tactic, Morgan employed an unusual strategy that would advantageously use the militia, the swales, and other topographical features of the land. He placed his troops on the field in a configuration unlike any that had been used by either army in this country. Morgan knew the militiamen, armed only with rifles, tended to run in the face of British bayonets; his strategy compensated for this typical militia behavior.

Morgan deployed his troops in three ranks. The first line consisted of militia sharpshooters under Colonel Pickens with orders to aim at the officers in the initial British charge and disrupt the command structure, a tactic that had proved successful at Musgrove Mill. Behind the sharpshooters were hundreds of South Carolina militiamen, including the Spartan and Fairforest Regiments, lined up across the road and extended some distance on either side. Behind them on the slope of a hill was the main battle line, consisting of the battle-tested Continentals from Virginia, Maryland, and Delaware, plus some militia from North Carolina and Virginia. Further back were Colonel William Washington's cavalrymen, 150 strong, arrayed out of sight on the left and right flanks, and ready to enter the fray to protect the flanks when warranted. Morgan's strategy was to lure Tarleton's men deeper into the web of Patriot forces, reducing their number at every advance.

During the pre-dawn hours before the battle began, Morgan walked through the camp to "spirit up the people" and inspire them for the coming fight. He explained how the military action would unfold. Knowing that the militia in the second line might run when they faced the British bayonet assault, he said to them: "All I want is for you to run where I tell you to run. I might need you again." He told them to fire at least two shots before moving behind the Continental line. Both Morgan and the militiamen knew the Broad River that lay behind them was swollen from the winter rain and would be difficult to cross. The militia had little choice but to stand and fight. With camp made and excitement in the air, Morgan and his men were ready for battle when Tarleton arrived about dawn.

Tarleton came to the Cowpens completely unaware of what lay ahead. The mixed British force of cavalry and infantry had been slogging through cold, rainy weather, battling flooding rivers for two weeks as they hunted and chased the Patriots through the backcountry. By January 17, the men were hungry, wet, and exhausted. Tarleton himself had not slept for two days. Upon reaching the battlefield, Tarleton could see only the first line of militiamen; the rest of the force was out of sight, a key to Morgan's strategy. In contrast, General Morgan mounted a horse, despite severe pain from his rheumatism, and took a position on a rise that enabled him to observe Tarleton's movements. When Tarleton attacked, he did not know whether Morgan was prepared to fight or if this was just a covering force to hold the British at bay while the main army escaped across the Broad River. With his judgment perhaps distorted from exhaustion and lack of sleep, the egotistical and overconfident Tarleton failed to discern Morgan's true intent.

Tarleton ordered the first wave of dragoons to advance toward Morgan's position before all his men had arrived on the field. As they did so, the militia sharpshooters' rifle fire killed about one-fourth of the mounted troops. Their duty completed, the sharpshooters dropped back to join Pickens' militia line. Tarleton deployed his units on the battlefield as they appeared on the Green River Road, not realizing the formation of the Patriot force. Once the battle was underway, everything favored the Patriots until the troops on the back line, one of the Continental units from Virginia, either did not hear or got confused about an order. Colonel John Eager Howard of the Continental Army ordered the Virginia Continentals to wheel to protect the flank from a concerted assault by the 71st Highlanders, a Scots infantry regiment of the British army. The Continentals misunderstood the order and began to withdraw. In the confusion, noise, and smoke, other units saw the Continentals abandon their position in the line and thought all units had been ordered to withdraw, so the third line, Morgan's major line, pulled out in a disciplined retreat.

Morgan yelled to Colonel Howard (who later became the governor of Maryland), "Are you defeated, sir?" Howard responded: "Look at these men, do they look like they are defeated?" Morgan told Howard that he was going to point to a place in the ground and "that's where I want your men to stop and fire."

As they retreated up a slight hill, the Continentals recharged their weapons. Morgan pointed to the place where he wanted Howard's group to turn and fire as one. Thinking the Patriots were retreating, the British lost all discipline, refused to obey Tarleton's order to charge the Patriots, and began a confused pursuit. The Patriots turned and fired, as Morgan had instructed, taking the British completely unawares. Morgan regrouped his unit and sent Pickens's militiamen around on the right flank of the British force and William Washington's Continentals around on the left in a double envelopment of Tarleton's men.

Morgan had trapped most of Tarleton's army, and the British position was almost hopeless. Still, Tarleton attempted to reassemble his men and direct the last minutes of the battle in person. His effort failed, and the British suffered a devastating defeat. In a battle that lasted less than an hour, 110 British soldiers perished, while only 12 Patriots were killed. Morgan captured about 500 prisoners. Tarleton himself barely escaped, and those in his command who had not been killed, captured, or wounded fled down the road toward Cornwallis. The British general, confident that Tarleton could defeat Morgan, was already on the way to North Carolina when he learned of the disaster at Cowpens. Morgan led his men toward Gilbert Town, and then northeast to Salisbury where he left the prisoners taken at Cowpens.

The Patriots had inflicted significant damage to Tarleton's army, Cornwallis's most mobile and valuable force. The victory was a coup for the Patriots because Tarleton was the best tactical officer the British had in the South. They feared him because of his military skill and also his ruthlessness and cruelty in battle and in the aftermath of battle. Whipping Tarleton and his crack British regulars was a powerful morale booster for the Patriots. The military strategy that Morgan employed at Cowpens was so successful that General

Nathanael Greene adapted its use in subsequent battles—at Hobkirk's Hill near Camden, Guilford Courthouse in North Carolina, and Eutaw Springs, for example.

In North Carolina, Morgan joined General Greene, but plagued by rheumatism and chronic malaria, he retired to his home in Virginia. Nathanael Greene added to his stellar reputation as a commander by wreaking havoc on the British at Guilford Courthouse, Ninety Six, and Eutaw Springs, where the last major battle of the Revolutionary War in South Carolina occurred. Cornwallis continued his march in North Carolina and Virginia, reaching Yorktown, Virginia, in October 1781, where he surrendered and most of the military actions of the war ended.

Although Cowpens was the last major battle in the Spartan District, the hatred and suspicions that Patriots and Loyalists had for each other persisted. As the Revolution continued, tensions escalated and allegiances changed, sometimes more than once, making it difficult to ascertain the number of Patriots and Loyalists in South Carolina. Daniel Plummer, for example, participated in the early military actions of the Patriot Spartan Regiment under Colonel Thomas Brandon. Around 1776, Plummer joined the Loyalist militia, and his men elected him major. James

Vernon, Plummer's neighbor, followed a similar course. After being driven from his home by the Patriots, Vernon joined a Loyalist militia regiment. Even in the wake of the Loyalist disaster at Kings Mountain, Vernon tried to keep his regiment together so that they might have another opportunity to defend the King. Golding Tinsley, who achieved some notoriety during the conflicts at Musgrove Mill and Blackstock's Plantation, was in the mounted ranger regiment. The Tinsleys were newcomers to the Spartan District, settling near Fairforest Creek in 1771. Two of Tinsley's brothers died during the war. Tories killed them. No one questioned Tinsley's loyalty to the Patriot cause.

For both Patriots and Loyalists during the war, maintaining military strength required living off the land. Consequently, both sides committed acts of thievery and sometimes even murder as they raided homes to obtain food, livestock, and other necessities. When a band of Loyalist raiders came into her home in the Irish Settlement on Fairforest Creek, Nancy Jackson kicked one of them down the steps. The Loyalists threatened her, and she fled to the home of relatives. In December 1780, Patriots seized Loyalist David George's wagons and horses. They thought George, who lived near the Tyger River, had spied for Cornwallis.

Among the Patriots captured at Blackstock's was William Hodge, who lived along the Pacolet River. Tarleton marched the prisoners toward Camden, and en route, forced Hodge to watch as the British troops killed his livestock and set fire to his house. Although his son-in-law was a Loyalist, Hodge served in the Fairforest Regiment under Colonel Thomas Brandon. He managed to escape from jail, rejoin his regiment, and participate in the Battle at Cowpens.

The British cause was clearly lost, but the allegiance of many South Carolina Loyalists remained strong. In the closing days of the Revolution, bitterness and rancor had not abated, and men on both sides committed acts of brutality and revenge. The fractiousness between Patriots and Loyalists in the backcountry gave William Cunningham and his followers an excuse to seek revenge, or, as Patriots believed, simply to commit criminal acts.

William Cunningham, who is remembered as the infamous "Bloody Bill" of the Revolutionary era, began his military career as a Patriot and participated in Williamson's Cherokee expeditions. Other members of his extended family were resolute in their loyalty to the King when the war broke out. Soon Cunningham abandoned the Patriot cause, not because of a change in political conviction, but because of a desire for personal vengeance. In addition to a disagreement over the terms of his military obligation, Cunningham learned that a Patriot had abused his father and beaten his lame and epileptic brother to death. He retaliated by murdering the perpetrator of the crime, perhaps an indication of what was to come. Later, in 1780 when the British controlled the backcountry, he joined his brother Patrick's Loyalist regiment and then assumed informal leadership of a group of fellow Loyalists. In 1781, Cunningham's gang began an independent campaign to reestablish the King's power in the backcountry. In mid-November, at Cloud's Creek in the Saluda District, Cunningham's men murdered 28 Patriots; only two of the Patriot militiamen survived. Two days later, at Hayes Station near Laurens, about 300 Loyalists under Cunningham slaughtered 18 Patriot militiamen and captured six— after they had surrendered. The stories of the abuses of Cunningham and his men spread quickly throughout the backcountry, and heightened the fears of all Patriots.

Cunningham's rampage through the backcountry lasted from November 10 to December 26, 1781. In their meanderings, Cunningham's men burned houses and barns, stole cattle and other livestock, and murdered those who were associated with the Patriot effort. Eventually, Cunningham and his men arrived in the Spartan District, where they headed to the Moore plantation at Walnut Grove. The Moore family were well-known Patriots, including Thomas Moore and Andrew and Kate Barry, all of whom had been active in the Patriot cause. In November 1781, the Moores were caring for an ailing Patriot officer, Captain Steadman. On a day when two of Steadman's friends were visiting him, Cunningham's horsemen stormed into the yard. The visitors ran, but the Loyalists murdered them as they fled. When they found Captain Steadman upstairs in bed, they killed him on the spot. In the first moments of the raid, Kate Barry slipped away and rode for help. She located her husband, Andrew, who led his militia regiment to Walnut Grove, arriving just in time to prevent the Loyalists from burning the house.

After the affair at Walnut Grove, Cunningham dragged James Wood, Commissioner of Sequestered Property, from his house. As he lay wounded outside the house, his wife begged the Loyalists to spare her husband's life, but they hanged him. Wood lived on Lawson's Fork, just west of the Enoree River and just beyond the boundary of the Spartan District. His brother, John, lived nearby. Cunningham and his men shot John Wood after he surrendered. The renegade Loyalist band torched several buildings that destroyed the Wofford's Ironworks and murdered John Snoddy. Many of Cunningham's victims were Patriot militiamen, including John Nuckolls, who owned land along Thicketty Creek and had been a militia captain.

Although the South Carolina General Assembly placed a bounty on Cunningham's head, no one captured him. He made his way to Florida, where he had lived at one time during the war, and from there moved to the Bahamas, where he died.

After Yorktown, British troops still occupied several important American garrisons, including Charleston. It took several months for the British to plan and execute their evacuation of Charleston; they did not leave the city until December 1782. Loyalists were concerned about whether or not British officials would simply abandon them, but their fears were unfounded. The British provided ships to evacuate Loyalists who wished to leave, not to escape capture, but to continue living under British rule. A few went to England. Others made their way to Florida or Canada, and a number of southern Loyalists made new lives in the British territories of the Caribbean. The new South Carolina government passed a confiscation act to seize the property of prominent Loyalists who had supported the King. The British government offered partial reimbursement to some Loyalists who lost property due to their allegiance to the Crown. Even so, some of the Loyalists remained in the new United States.

Some Loyalists left the Carolinas before the war ended, including James Miller, who lived on the Pacolet River in the Spartan District and feared reprisals from his Patriot neighbors. Zacharias Gibbes, commander of the Loyalist militia in the area of the Spartan District, visited Jamaica but then settled in Canada's Maritime Provinces. Daniel Plummer, seriously wounded at Kings Mountain, moved to Florida. Alexander Chesney, who lived in the area of Grindal Shoals and whose journal is an important source for the study of the American Revolution, returned to Ireland.

Thomas Fletchall was one of those targeted by the new state government's confiscation acts, and he resettled in Jamaica. The state seized his property and sold it at auction. Thomas Brandon, colonel of the Fairforest militia, bought Fletchall's extensive estate at a nominal price because no one bid against him.

With the end of the war, tranquility came to the Spartan District. Now part of a new state in a new nation, the men and women of the Spartan District returned to making a living on their farms. The first United States Census, taken in 1790, attempted to provide an accurate accounting of the nation's population. The data for the "Spartanburg sub-district of the Ninety Six District" records a population of a little more than 9,000. In addition, the census documented 827 slaves. Most people in the district did not own slaves. The majority of those who did had fewer than five slaves, and most of them had only one slave. At the time of the census, William Thomson had the largest number of slaves, 27. Business enterprises continued to develop, including a tavern, general store and post office operated by Thomas and Ann Price at their home. However, small-scale agriculture still dominated the economy of the area; cotton had not yet become the major crop of South Carolina.

Revolutionary War Patriot leaders from the Spartan District continued to represent the people in the District after the war. Thomas Brandon and John Thomas Jr., for example, served in the new state legislature. One of the first acts of this legislature partitioned the old Ninety Six District into counties in 1785, partly to facilitate legal activities. The establishment of a court system in the same year resolved some of the issues that had divided the district before and during the Revolutionary period. The first court meeting of the newly created Spartanburg County occurred at Nicholl's Mill (now called Anderson Mill) on the Tyger River. Thomas Williamson offered two acres of land in the middle of the new county for the court house and jail, and local commissioners, including Bayliss Earle and John Thomas Jr., purchased adjacent acreage that became the nucleus of the village of Spartanburg. Later known as Morgan Square, this area was the county's commercial center. The town of Spartanburg, however, was not incorporated until 1831.

Thomas Jefferson called the battles at Kings Mountain and Cowpens "the joyful annunciation of that turn in the tide of success which terminated the war with the seal of independence." Those successes would not have occurred without the valiant actions of the Patriots of the Spartan District who, during the summer of 1780, fought for the cause of independence. This required them to fight their neighbors and sometimes family members. It required good Christians to engage in murderous and sometimes unspeakable acts. It was not easy, this turning point that brought forth a new nation unlike any the world had ever known. ■

ABOUT THE AUTHORS

KATHERINE DAVIS CANN

Katherine Davis Cann is Professor of History and Chair of the Social Science Department at Spartanburg Methodist College. She is a graduate of Lander University and holds advanced degrees from the University of North Carolina (MA in History) and the University of South Carolina (PhD in History).

Her essay, "Improving Textile Town, 1910-1929," appeared in *Textile Town: Spartanburg, SC* (Hub City Press, 2002) and her study entitled "Freedmen and Schools in Abbeville County, 1865-1875," was published as a chapter in *Recovering the Piedmont Past: Unexplored Moments in Nineteenth Century Upcountry South Carolina History* (USC Press, 2013). Dr. Cann is the author of *Common Ties: A History of Textile Industrial Institute, Spartanburg Junior College, and Spartanburg Methodist College* published by Hub City Press.

GEORGE FIELDS

George Fields is a retired United Methodist minister who served as a pastor, an Army Chaplain rising to rank of Brigadier General, and president of Spartanburg Methodist College. He spends his retirement years researching and preserving Revolutionary War battlefields in South Carolina. He provided leadership in preserving twelve sites, serving as the Military Heritage Director of Palmetto Conservation Foundation.

SELECTED BIBLIOGRAPHY

Bailey, Rev. J. D. *History of Grindal Shoals and Some Early Adjacent Families* (Gaffney: The Ledger Press, 1927).

Buchanan, John. *The Road to Guilford Courthouse: The American Revolution in the Carolinas* (New York: John Wiley & Sons, 1997).

Cann, Marvin L. *"Ninety Six—A History of the Backcountry, 1700-1781."* unpublished mss. 1972.

Draper, Lyman Copeland. *King's Mountain and Its Heroes: History of the Battle of King's Mountain, October 7th, 1780, and the Events Which Led to It.* (Cincinnati: P. G. Thomson, 1881).

Edgar, Walter. *Partisans and Redcoats: The Southern Conflict That Turned the Tide of the American Revolution* (New York: Perennial, 2001).

Edgar, Walter. *The South Carolina Encyclopedia* (Columbia: University of South Carolina Press, 2006)

Fields, George D., Jr. *"The Battle of Blackstock's."* unpublished mss., n.d.

Fields, George D., Jr. Revolutionary War Tour in the Spartanburg Area. unpublished mss., n.d.

Fields, George D., Jr. Author's interviews, March 29, August 3, September 18, 2013, in Spartanburg, SC.

Fischer, David Hackett. *Albion's Seed: Four British Folkways in America* (New York: Oxford University Press, 1986).

Gibbes, Robert W. *Documentary History of the American Revolution: Consisting of Letters and Papers Relating to the Contest for Liberty, Chiefly in South Carolina, from Originals in Possession of the Editor and Other Sources* (New York: D. Appleton & Co, 1853).

Graves, William T. *James Williams: An American Patriot in the Carolina Backcountry* (San Jose, CA: Writers' Club Press, 2003).

Hope, Wes. *The Spartanburg Area in the American Revolution* (Spartanburg: Altman Printing Co., Inc., 2003).

Howe, George D. *History of the Presbyterian Church in South Carolina*, vol. I (New York: Duffie & Chapman, 1870).

Lambert, Robert Stansbury. *South Carolina Loyalists in the American Revolution* (Columbia: University of South Carolina Press, 1987).

Moss, Bobby Gilmer, ed. *Journal of Capt. Alexander Chesney: Adjutant to Major Patrick Ferguson* (Blacksburg, SC: Scotia-Hibernia Press, 2002).

Moss, Bobby Gilmer. *The Loyalists at King's Mountain* (Blacksburg, SC: Scotia-Hibernia Press, 1998).

Moss, Bobby Gilmer, ed. *Uzal Johnson, Loyalist Surgeon: A Revolutionary War Diary* (Blacksburg, SC: Scotia-Hibernia Press, 2000).

The State (Columbia, South Carolina). June 30, 1940.

Townsend, Leah. *South Carolina Baptists, 1670-1805* (Baltimore: Genealogical Publishing Co., 1974).

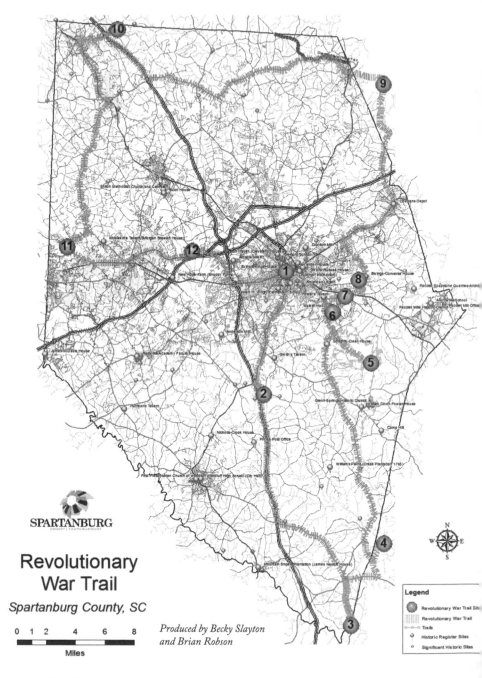

![SPARTANBURG COUNTY | SOUTH CAROLINA]

Revolutionary
War Trail

Spartanburg County, SC

0 1 2   4   6   8

Miles

*Produced by Becky Slayton
and Brian Robson*

Legend

Revolutionary War Trail Site
Revolutionary War Trail
Trails
Historic Register Sites
Significant Historic Sites

VISIT THE SPARTANBURG AREA REVOLUTIONARY WAR TRAIL

The Revolutionary War Trail is a driving tour of key historic spots in the Spartanburg area that played a part in the victory for the American side. Each stop has a historic plaque with in-depth information. The trail, which opened in fall 2014, is a project of the Spartanburg Convention & Visitors Bureau in conjunction with the Spartanburg County Historical Association.

1. Daniel Morgan Monument

The Daniel Morgan Monument was erected in the City of Spartanburg in 1881 for the centennial of the Battle of Cowpens by the original 13 colonies and Tennessee. It was the first joint effort of these states following the Civil War. The monument has become a symbol of Spartanburg and its Revolutionary War heritage.

Location: Morgan Square, downtown Spartanburg (Corner of Main and Magnolia streets).

2. Walnut Grove Plantation

Walnut Grove Plantation is the pre-Revolutionary home of the Charles Moore family. The home was raided by "Bloody Bill" Cunningham in 1781 and was the childhood home of Kate Moore Barry, a scout for the Patriots prior to the Battle of Cowpens. The site is operated by the Spartanburg County Historical Association (spartanburghistory.org). The home and grounds are open to the public seasonally and staff is available for tours; the site also includes a picnic shelter, restrooms, office and gift shop.

Location: 1200 Otts Shoals Road, Roebuck, near Interstate 26 Exit 28 (SC Highway 211, SE of Spartanburg).

3. The Battle of Musgrove Mill

At this site a small force of frontier militia defeated a larger joint force of Loyalist militia and British Provincial Regulars on August 19, 1780. This site is part of a state park with interpretive trails, a visitor center, restrooms and a full-time staff.

Location: 398 State Park Road, Clinton, 29325, along SC Highway 56 and the bridge over the Enoree River at the juncture of Spartanburg, Laurens and Union counties. (southcarolinaparks.com/musgrovemill)

4. The Battle of Blackstock's

General Thomas Sumter and American militia defeated Lieutenant Colonel Banastre Tarleton and a small detachment of British Regulars at this site on November 20, 1780. The battlefield is protected public property and is accessible by vehicle. There is an information kiosk, small parking area, battle monument and a spur of the Palmetto Trail along the Tyger River here.

Location: Just off of Blackstock Road on the Tyger River near SC Highway 56. (southcarolinaparks.com/musgrovemill)

5. The Battle of Kelso Creek

In 1780 a force of Loyalists attacked the house of Colonel John Thomas where ammunition was being stored for the Patriots. The attack was repulsed and the ammunition was removed to a safe location.

Location: 450 Croft State Park Road, Spartanburg, 29302. The Thomas home site is located near the junction of Fairforest Creek and Kelsey Creek inside of Croft State Park. The exact location is not safely accessible. (southcarolinaparks.com/croft)

6. The Battle of Cedar Spring

At this site, a British force planned to attack an American militia force camped at Cedar Spring on July 12, 1780. The militia had heard of the planned attack and ambushed the British forces instead.

Location: 140 Cedar Springs Place, Spartanburg 29302. The spring is on land owned by the South Carolina School for the Deaf and the Blind (scsdb.org) near the Palmetto Trail (palmettoconservation.org) below Cedar Spring Baptist Church.

7. The Battle of the Peach Trees

On August 8, 1780, along the Georgia Road, the British had been delayed all morning by the leapfrogging Patriot defensive position. The Patriots gathered a larger force and pushed the retreating enemy down the road. In the early afternoon Colonel Patrick Ferguson arrived with reinforcements and pushed the Patriots back toward the Wofford Iron Works on Lawson's Fork Creek.

Location: Intersection of Dogwood Club Road and Old Petrie Road Extension, near Southport Road (SC Hwy 295), Spartanburg, 29302. The site is on private property and has been heavily developed.

8. The Battle of Wofford's Iron Works

This is the site of an early ironworking operation established by the SC Government during the American Revolution. Part of a running battle occurred here on August 8, 1780 between frontier militia forces and British Loyalists and Provincial regulars. This running battle is referred to by several names, including "2nd

Cedar Spring," "The Battle of the Peach Trees," and "The Battle of Wofford's Iron Works."

Location: Near the intersection of Clifton-Glendale Road and Emma Cudd Road, on Lawson's Fork Creek near the present day Glendale Mill site at the blueway put-in. The precise battle/iron works sites are not known.

9. The Battle of Cowpens

General Daniel Morgan and a joint force of American militia and Continental regulars bested Lieutenant Colonel Banastre Tarleton here on January 17, 1781. This is a National Park with visitor center, interpretive trails, recreational facilities, restrooms, and a full-time staff.

Location: SC Hwy 11, 4001 Chesnee Highway, Gaffney, SC 29341. (nps. gov/cowp)

10. The Battle of Earle's Ford

Located near the town of Landrum, this is the site of a Loyalist attack on a Patriot encampment on July 15, 1780, in which the Patriot forces were able to repel the Loyalist attack.

Location: There is a granite DAR marker commemorating the action on SC Highway 14 just off of Interstate 26 in Landrum (at the Four Columns house). The actual ford site is on

the North Pacolet River east of the monument on private property.

11. Wood's Fort

Wood's Fort, which no longer exists, was a pre-Revolutionary War fort built along the Indian boundary line (Greenville-Spartanburg County line). It protected the families in the area during the war with the Cherokees in 1775 and 1776. The structure was re-fortified in 1780.

Location: 1915 Gap Creek Road, Greer, SC 29651. There is a monument off US Highway 29 near the junction of Road 908 and SC Highway 357 near Apalache Baptist Church.

12. The Battle of Fort Prince

Fort Prince was one of several pre-Revolutionary War forts built near the Indian boundary line that also were used during the Revolution. The British were driven from the fort by Patriots on July 16, 1780. There is a roadside monument in a copse of oak trees near where the fort once stood. Access requires parking on the side of the road and walking through a private residential area.

Location: Located just off of Fort Prince Road, 29385, not far from Interstate 85 and US Highway 29 near Lyman.

INDEX

HUB CITY PRESS

Hub City Press is an independent press in Spartanburg, South Carolina, that publishes well-crafted, high-quality works by new and established authors, with an emphasis on the Southern experience. We are committed to high-caliber novels, short stories, poetry, plays, memoir, and works emphasizing regional culture and history. We are particularly interested in books with a strong sense of place.

Hub City Press is an imprint of the non-profit Hub City Writers Project, founded in 1995 to foster a sense of community through the literary arts. Our metaphor of organization purposely looks backward to the nineteenth century when Spartanburg was known as the "hub city," a place where railroads converged and departed.

HUB CITY SPARTANBURG HISTORY TITLES

Because Memory Isn't Eternal ~ Deno Trakas
Come to the Cow Pens! ~ Christine Swager
Common Ties ~ Katherine Cann
Courageous Kate ~ Sheila Ingle
Family Trees: The Peach Culture of the Piedmont ~ Mike Corbin
Fearless Martha ~ Sheila Ingle
Hub City Music Makers ~ Peter Cooper
Magical Places ~ Marion Peter Holt
Seeing Spartanburg ~ Philip N. Racine
South of Main ~ Brenda Lee and Beatrice Hill
Spartanburg Revisited ~ Emily Smith et al
Textile Town ~ Betsy Wakefield Teter, editor
When the Soldiers Came to Town ~ Susan Turpin et al
Where Champions Play ~ Jason Gilmer